Fires of Pentecost
on the Battlefront

Quiet Power - Breakthrough Results

Jim Kilmer

TEACH Services, Inc.
PUBLISHING
www.TEACHServices.com • (800) 367-1844

All Scriptures, unless otherwise stated, are taken from the New King James Version®. Copyright © 1982 by Thomas Nelson. Used by permission. All rights reserved.

Scripture quotations marked KJV are from the King James Version of the Holy Bible.

Scripture taken from the New American Standard Bible®. Copyright © 1960, 1962, 1963, 1968, 1971, 1972, 1973, 1975, 1977, 1995 by The Lockman Foundation. Used by permission.

Scripture quotations marked (NLT) are taken from the Holy Bible, New Living Translation, copyright © 1996, 2004, 2007, 2013, 2015 by Tyndale House Foundation. Used by permission of Tyndale House Publishers, Inc., Carol Stream, Illinois 60188. All rights reserved.

World rights reserved. This book or any portion thereof may not be copied or reproduced in any form or manner whatever, except as provided by law, without the written permission of the publisher, except by a reviewer who may quote brief passages in a review.

The author assumes full responsibility for the accuracy of all facts and quotations as cited in this book. The opinions expressed in this book are the author's personal views and interpretations, and do not necessarily reflect those of the publisher.

This book is provided with the understanding that the publisher is not engaged in giving spiritual, legal, medical, or other professional advice. If authoritative advice is needed, the reader should seek the counsel of a competent professional.

Copyright © 2018 Jim Kilmer
Copyright © 2018 TEACH Services, Inc.
ISBN-13: 978-1-4796-0894-2 (Paperback)
ISBN-13: 978-1-4796-0895-9 (ePub)
Library of Congress Control Number: 2018937819

Published by

www.TEACHServices.com • (800) 367-1844

*This book is dedicated to Burton Maxwell,
a man who taught me to pray,
and to the hundreds of soul winners that the Lord
has allowed me to work with through the years.*

Table of Contents

Endorsements 7
Preface 9
1. *Breaking the Guilt Complex* 13
2. *Witnessing and the Heebie-Jeebies* . .15
3. *Big Moe* 18
4. *Why Jesus Was Sometimes Silent* . . .22
5. *God Takes the Reins* 27
6. *Praying for Other People's Success; Dramatic Answers* 30
7. *Work with Interested People* 34
8. *Word in Season Opportunities* . . .36
9. *Cooperating with Angels* 39
10. *God Uses Those Who Recognize Their Need* 42
11. *Ask for the Baptism of the Holy Spirit* .44
12. *Experiencing God's Presence* 47
13. *Cautions Regarding the Baptism of the Holy Spirit* 49
14. *Spared by the Spirit from Unknown Tongues* 52
15. *The Gifts of the Spirit in Operation* . .55
16. *Soul Winning through Spiritual Gifts* . .58
17. *Holy Spirit and Joy* 63
18. *When No One Seems Interested* . . .65
19. *Using the Right Tools* 70
20. *How to Give Bible Studies* 74
21. *Mining Gold and Holding the Nugget* . 78
22. *Quotes on Prayer* 81
23. *The Baptism of the Holy Spirit* . . .83
24. *Cleansing Fire and New Creation* . . 85
25. *Eyewitness Account of the Upper Room Experience* . . .88
26. *Baptism of the Holy Spirit and the Latter Rain* 91
27. *The Promise of the Spirit Fulfilled* . . 94
28. *Baptism of the Holy Spirit and Speaking in Tongues* 96
29. *Prayer That Reaches Souls for Christ* . 98
30. *The Plague of Being Human* . . . 103
31. *More Powerful than Bullets* . . . 107
32. *Fires of Pentecost on the Battlefront* . 109
33. *Getting Past the KGB* 112
34. *When the Rain Didn't Stop* . . . 115
35. *Key Texts and Quotes: The Baptism of the Holy Spirit and Witnessing (KJV)* . 117

Supplements
(available online at jimkilmer.com)
1. Gospel Presentation
2. Reaching Missing Members
3. Sabbath School Action Units Plan in Brief
4. Integrating New Members into the Life of the Church
5. Your Personal Witness
6. Spiritual Gifts Inventory

Endorsements

After reading the manuscript, Dr. George Knight, well known author and retired professor of Church History at Andrews University said:

> Jim is absolutely correct that nearly all believers feel awkward when it comes to witnessing to others. What they need is not more guilt, but practical solutions. The manuscript provides solutions in a manner that addresses both their hopes and fears. Particularly helpful are the many stories from real life that engage readers and draw them into the flow of the book (Letter of recommendation, May 22, 2015).

> Jim, your theology of the baptism of the Holy Spirit is right on. And so is the relationship with the baptism and witnessing and the Christian life. The manuscript is very practical and written in down home on the farm type of language that will speak to the average lay person. The flow and progression of the presentation is good and logical. And the title is excellent (email, May 14, 2015).

Kurt Johnson, director of Voice of Prophecy Bible School, said:

> Hi Jim, I read your book…very good job! It is inspirational and instructional. The stories cause you to respond…hey, I can do this! (email).

Dr. Joseph Kidder, professor at Andrews University Theological Seminary:

> I read the Manuscript. It is great work. Please submit it for publication. Many people will benefit from it (email).

Max Torkelsen, retired President of the North Pacific Union Conference of Seventh-day Adventists:

> Jim Kilmer's book, *Fires of Pentecost on the Battlefront*, not only tells us *why* we need the Holy Spirit's power, *but also* explains clearly and carefully *how* to experience the baptism of the Holy Spirit. Kilmer makes things practical by using illustrations from his own experience here in the United States and overseas in Beruit, Lebanon and in the former Soviet Union where he led and organized the door-to-door distribution of 100,000 copies of the book *Desire of Ages*. I enjoyed his sometimes-unexpected turn of phrase in chapter headings like "Witnessing and the Heebie-Jeebies" and "The Big Moe." I highly recommend this volume that reminds us of the pivotal role of the Holy Spirit in winning souls and preparing for the soon return of Jesus.

Preface

Ron Clouzet's book, *Adventism's Greatest Need,* proclaims that the baptism of the Holy Spirit and latter rain are now available to God's people. The book you are holding in your hand, *Fires of Pentecost on the Battlefront,* follows with practical application. The book does not attempt to assign more work or offer contrived formulas, but to open eyes to see how God is working and show how to cooperate with Him to win souls.

Insights for effective conversational evangelism are taken from the model of Jesus' daily baptism of the Holy Spirit. True stories illustrate these simple principles. The events have taken place much the way they are reported. Most names have been changed in order to maintain the privacy of those involved.

Some reports are from actual battlefield experiences in Beirut, Lebanon. Others are from the arena of spiritual conflict in the former Soviet Union, but most have taken place in the United States. These experiences could happen to any one of us. They demonstrate that great miracles can occur within our own sphere of influence, and that we don't have to wait for some time in the future to receive the latter rain.

After Pentecost, the disciples met in small companies and studied the teaching of the apostles, prayed together, ministered to each other, reached out to others, and continued to multiply in numbers. Small groups and soul-winning Sabbath school classes should find this volume to be a ready guide to experience power and instruction for witnessing.

It is assumed that the reader will have familiarity with the writings of Ellen G. White, referenced throughout the book. These writings are available at https://egwwritings.org/ and at Adventist Book Centers. Supplemental materials referenced may be accessed Online at jimkilmer.com.

This is my desire:
"Now that I am old and gray,
do not abandon me, O God.
Let me proclaim
your power to this new generation,
your mighty miracles
to all who come after me."

(Ps. 71:18, NLT)

Chapter 1
Breaking the Guilt Complex

"Win a soul or face eternal damnation. That's the idea I get." With tight lips and troubled brow, Carl poured out his frustrations. "Neither my wife nor I can point to a single person we have brought to the Lord." After squirming in his seat for an hour during seemingly superhuman testimonies, Carl sank lower in his chair at camp meeting. Already feeling ashamed, he could not believe what he heard. The preacher strongly implied that we won't be in heaven unless we have a soul we have won to meet us there.

Carl was not alone with his tormented conscience when it comes to successful witnessing. The church in North America has little if any kingdom growth apart from those who enter from other countries. Yet the fact remains that disciples of Jesus are commissioned to make more disciples, and a church without mission is no church at all.

The less often members experience success in soulwinning, the more often leaders and writers are prone to promotion. Bible class facilitators customarily wrap up their studies with the admonition to witness, and pious members nod in agreement. However, most members know they are not doing what a disciple should do. Pressures mount. Members like Carl get discouraged. Spiritual rigor mortis sets in and more and more of them stay away from church. If they continue to attend, more likely than not, lay members will reach an overwhelming level of guilt. Having given up in frustration, they simply go home for their "lay activities" after potluck.

To make matters worse, unbelievers these days seem hostile to spiritual talk unless it tickles their fancy.

The baptism of the Holy Spirit promises to change all this. True stories in this book will demonstrate how you can witness in the Holy Spirit. Experiencing the thrill of bringing souls to Christ is easier than you might think. The Holy Spirit will make ministry joyous and give power to your witness. Profound soulwinning miracles are taking place through humble gospel workers and lay members like you, and this is happening in spite of a society that is gripped by spiritual darkness.

God often works in the most dramatic manner in the midst of turmoil, upheaval, and chaos. He is

> *God often works in the most dramatic manner in the midst of turmoil, upheaval, and chaos.*

not limited in what He can do. It simply becomes more necessary that He Himself takes the reins. Sometimes the raw reality of basic survival can teach us to depend totally on God. His miracles are real, and through the promised Holy Spirit, He has power to save to the uttermost those that come to Him.

God works through common people, filled with the Holy Spirit. The whole world is yet to be enlightened through real people like you and me who have been filled with the Holy Spirit.

The following chapters will demonstrate how:

- The Holy Spirit is drawing souls to Himself.

- God will help you find those who are being drawn.

- We make the work of winning souls ten times more difficult than it needs be by failing to cooperate with the Holy Spirit.

- You need not try to convince a person who is not receptive, or spend time arguing with one who does not want to learn.

- We may need to say less, rather than more, when reaching the lost.

- The greatest opportunities for soulwinning often lie within the circles of our daily lives.

- Angels will lead us to those who are longing for light.

- The baptism of the Holy Spirit will enable you to win souls while minimizing fear, coercion, and contrived formulas.

To be filled with the Holy Spirit is not a frightening thing; it is not fanaticism. It does not make people "so heavenly minded that they become of no earthly good." Walking in the Spirit is wholesome, practical, joyous, fulfilling, and doable.

Carl and his wife experienced a simple, Spirit-filled way to bear fruit in soulwinning, and you may also.

Chapter 2
Witnessing and the Heebie-Jeebies

The literature evangelist trainer, Rod, took a trainee, Ben, door-to-door to canvass for Christian literature. Rod demonstrated the approach a number of times. He rang the bell, and when the resident responded, he started out by saying, "Hi, I am Rod and this Ben."

Then he went on explaining their mission. He repeated the same phrase a number of times until it was Ben's turn. Ben was understandably anxious and, as it turned out, had learned all too well.

When the woman came to the door, Ben blurted out, "Hi, I'm Rod" and, pointing to the real Rod, he said, "and this is Ben." Then Ben quickly caught himself. Nervously and still confused, he pointed again to Rod and shouted, "No! That isn't right. *He's* Ben and *I'm* Rod."

Fortunately, the woman at the door had a sense of humor and invited them in, saying, "Well why don't you come in and maybe you can figure out who you are."

From the comfort of one's armchair, it doesn't seem possible that anyone could get this flustered, yet most who have tried to witness will understand that the brain can easily get befuddled with fright. Witnessing does not have to generate the kind of fear experienced by Ben.

If ever there is a word that gives the common Christian the heebie-jeebies, it is the word "witnessing". Advertise a sermon on witnessing and don't be surprised if the pews are empty Sabbath morning. Yet, over and over in Bible study class, church members inflict guilt upon themselves for not witnessing. For the most part, the thought of witnessing renders shame rather than joy. This is a major problem because the task of the church and one great purpose of the Christian life is witnessing.

However, there are exciting solutions for overcoming our common bumbling attempts to witness. The Lord would have us live a life free from guilt. If anyone had more fear and trepidation than Ben did, it was the author of this book. This, however, drove me to my knees to prayerfully discover multiple methods and solutions that are real and can turn the bumbling witness into a powerful instrument in the hands of the Lord.

By the Lord's grace, I will set before the reader simple, practical methods that get results and can be experienced by anyone capable of prayer and surrender to God.

It all begins with a baptism of the Holy Spirit. The Holy Spirit brings a refreshing shower of heavenly blessings. Witnessing in the Spirit means letting God work the miracles while we simply yield mind, mouth, hands, and feet to His operation.

The Lord will lead the Spirit-filled witness to seekers through scores of avenues other than door-to-door witnessing, but even door-to-door witnessing can be joyous and productive when one follows the lead of the Holy Spirit. The same principle applies—namely, to look for those that are responding to the drawing of the Holy Spirit.

I know this is extreme, but it illustrates the point. My partner and I were visiting people who had once been involved in church, but were not currently attending. The front steps were high. A large man, swaying from side to side, silhouetted in the doorway. I claimed the promise for words to speak and opened my mouth, "I am not sure why we are here, but we are looking for those that the Holy Spirit has been speaking to."

"The Holy Spirit has been telling me that I should be keeping the Sabbath," he said.

I am not advocating this as a canvass, nor have I ever said it before or after, but it demonstrates the reality of the attitude we may have when going door-to-door or in conversational evangelism. I try to go with the attitude that we are looking for people with whom the Holy Spirit has been working.

On another occasion, I was visiting door-to-door, accompanied by a new member. We were telling people about Christian television and inviting them to participate in a spring Bible reading program. The people were very responsive. A woman met us at the gate. We told her what we were doing. She said we needed to speak with her husband, Corky. She invited us inside where Corky sat in a soft chair, smiling. I expected the Holy Spirit to lead in the conversation, so we simply sat in silence. Then I asked him where he saw the Lord leading him in his life. Corky responded, "I guess I am looking for a church."

We left Bible studies with him and continued on down the street. Around the corner of the block, a woman drove into her driveway, heading for her carport. She rolled her window down and we explained, "We are telling people about Christian television in this area."

We handed her a flier with pictures of Mark Finley and Doug Batchelor and said, "Along with this we are encouraging folks to participate in a spring community Bible reading program."

"I know all about it and I am not interested," she said as she drove on into the carport.

As she got out of her car, my partner said, "We were hoping you would join."

"I have been a Lutheran for thirty years and I am not going to become a Seventh-day Adventist," she said firmly as she walked toward her door.

I whispered to my partner, "That's a good sign." I knew that she had some knowledge of Bible truth and there must have been some conviction there for her to mention it.

"Oh no," I said, "He means he hopes you will join in the community Bible reading program."

"Oh well, I guess I could do that," she replied.

Edna was a great student of the Bible. She carefully filled out each lesson and invited us in to review her answers. "Did you know George Vandeman?" she inquired.

"Well I certainly knew who he was, but I didn't know him personally."

"We used to park our trailer next to him and go swimming with him and Millie. Do you know…" and she mentioned another prominent Seventh-day Adventist minister.

"Edna, you knew these folks better than I and I was raised in an Adventist home."

"Well there is more to the story. I used to be a Seventh-day Adventist. I was a Sabbath School superintendent in the _____ Church. My husband was not a church member. He had multiple affairs. I came to the point where I had had enough and filed for divorce. He went to my pastor and filled his ears with false stories. The pastor did not talk to me or visit. He sent me a letter letting me know that I had been dropped from membership. My son was at the church camp that summer. He gave his heart to the Lord and made a decision to be baptized. He came home and told me about it. It was very painful to show him the letter. That was thirty years ago."

We apologized profusely for this mistake on the part of the pastor and prayed together. We asked our conference president to write a letter of apology and offer to reinstate Edna into church membership.

She told us on our next visit that Corky had come by and said, "Mama, I think we better go to the Seventh-day Adventist Church this Sabbath."

Yes, Corky, the man down the street, was the boy who had made his decision at camp and never followed through after his mother received the letter of separation from the church.

Edna was in Sabbath School and church the following Sabbath. After the service, she asked one of the elders, "What do I need to do to become a member of this church?"

Now rewind a bit. Elder Bronson, a retired minister, cared for his invalid wife for years, waiting on her every need. Mrs. Bronson passed away and Elder Bronson was lonely. As he prayed, a picture popped into his mind of a young girl that he had admired in academy. He got out an old school annual (what we now call a yearbook) and looked up her name. He began to inquire about her. He found that she had recently rejoined the Seventh-day Adventist Church. He walked into Sabbath School and sat down next to—you guessed it—Edna. They were soon married and had a number of happy golden years together.

These stories illustrate the fact that the Holy Spirit can lead us to seekers even when going door-to-door, but as mentioned previously, most of the greatest opportunities for witnessing lie within our own sphere of influence as the Holy Spirit guides us to seekers through prayer and conversation. Witnessing in the Holy Spirit takes away the heebie-jeebies and replaces them with fullness of joy.

Chapter 3
Big Moe

How was Len supposed to know that Big Moe had been bouncing drunks out of his two taverns for much of the night? Moe was mad. "You call me again at this time of morning and I will call you at three o'clock in the morning when I get off work!"

Moe was one of the members of Len's motorcycle club. Len had called about club business. He apologized and acknowledged that it would not be fun to be awakened at 3 a.m. in the morning. Len called later in the afternoon and Moe was much more amenable. As they talked, Len silently prayed for Moe since he was a member of Len's *oikos*.

Oikos is the Greek word for "household". Praying for those within one's *oikos* is one of the primary aspects of soulwinning. In Greek and Roman times, *oikos* included the immediate family and extended to include others within one's sphere of influence (see page 67). The model of ministering first to one's *oikos* comes from Jesus. After he healed the man possessed of demons, He told him, "Return to your own house, and tell what great things God has done for you. And he went his way and proclaimed throughout the whole city what great things Jesus had done for him" (Luke 8:39). In that experience, the man's household either included or grew to be an entire city. There are two basic soulwinning principles in this passage: 1) Begin with your own household and circle of acquaintances and 2) Give your testimony concerning the great things God has done in your life.

One of the first things to do for those in need of the Savior is to pray for them. Jesus said, "If anyone sees his brother sinning a sin *which does* not *lead* to death, he will ask, and He will give him life…" (1 John 5:16). Circles of influence include extended family members and friends of family members. They include neighbors, work associates, service providers, and fraternities. Len prayed regularly for each member of his motorcycle club. As he prayed, his heart went out to Moe.

> ***One of the first things to do for those in need of the Savior is to pray for them.***

Len followed the counsel written through inspiration: "As we see souls out of Christ, we are to put ourselves in their place, and in their behalf feel repentance before God, resting not until we bring them to repentance" (White, *The SDA Bible Commentary*, Vol. 7, p. 960).

Len tried to put himself in Moe's place. In spite of his rough, direct manner, Len found himself appreciating Moe's honest, straightforward way of relating. Len was so secure and joyous in Jesus that he was not threatened by Moe's rough exterior. He thought, *'What if I were Moe? As Moe, what would I know about the Lord?'* Len began to feel great compassion. If he were Moe, he sensed that he would be lonely at heart and longing for a peace that this world cannot provide. He would be tired of the rude and crude ways of the bar crowd. He would be alarmed about the condition of his soul. Len prayed for Moe with strong emotion. He confessed, in Moe's behalf, a need for the Savior and to turn from an empty way of life.

Moe called one day and said that he needed to get out of the club. Len listened and expressed the fact that he was sorry to see him leave. Moe said that he was going through a divorce and would need to sell his motorcycle. Len, sensing what he would be feeling in that situation, turned immediately to God in Moe's behalf. Len wanted to say something to Moe about God, but knew the word spoken must be "in season." Words came to mind, but there was another conflicting thought that went something like this: *'You can't push religion on the men of the motorcycle club. Moe is a man of the world. He will not want your religious thoughts.'* However, there was another still small voice that whispered, "What if he wants to get out of his lifestyle?"

Len said, "Moe, I am a man of faith. I would like to say a prayer for you if that would be okay." All was quiet on the other end of the phone.

Moe finally said, "I know God is important, but right now I think He is ticked off at me."

Len told Moe that God does not relate to us the way we relate to one another. "We naturally think that God would treat us the way we treat Him, but this is not the case. God takes all the trash that we throw in His face and gives us love in return." Len prayed a brief prayer for Moe and his wife.

"Our Creator God, Your word says concerning Moe and Christy, 'I have loved you with everlasting love, therefore with loving kindness have I drawn you. Fear not, for I have redeemed you, I have called you by your name,' Moe. 'You are mine. When you pass through the waters I will be with you and through the rivers they shall not overflow you. I will be with you; yes I will uphold you with the right hand of my righteousness.'" Moe thanked Len for the prayer.

Len continued to pray for Moe. After several weeks they talked again. Moe said that he and his wife had reconciled and were back together. They had closed the doors on their taverns. Neither Moe nor his wife wanted to be around the tavern crowd any longer. In a calm, friendly voice, Len asked if they had Christians with whom to fellowship. Moe said that he had been attending a certain church, but was looking for a different church to attend. He asked, "Where do you go to church?"

Len and Moe made arrangements to worship together. Len eagerly looked forward to taking Moe to church. He had a class in mind where Moe would not feel out of place. Things came up and Moe was not able to meet the various appointments they made. Len did not want to badger Moe, but knew that the Holy Spirit was working on Moe's heart. He continued to claim promises in his behalf.

After several more weeks of praying for Moe, Len decided to call him and offer to let him ride one of his motorcycles. Moe's first response when he heard Len's voice was, "We need to go to church. Are you coming to my church or do I have to go to your church?" He told Len that he had a Seventh-day Adventist friend and they had discussed the importance of the seventh-day Sabbath.

Len said, "I go to church on Saturday, the seventh-day Sabbath."

Moe and his wife Christy met Len and his wife Lorraine at church that Sabbath. Christy discovered that her physical therapist was a member of that church. Moe and Christy attended again, on their own. Moe expressed interest in studying Bible prophecy.

I am convinced that we have scarcely scratched the surface of experiencing the fruits of the righteous man that accomplishes much in intercessory prayer.

Heartfelt intercessory prayer answers the argument of Satan and reclaims souls who have fallen into sin. The Bible is full of stories, parables, illustrations, and promises of how intercessory prayer delivers those held captive by Satan.

For a deeper understanding of intercessory prayer and amazing stories and promises, read chapters 22 and 29.

1. John 6:44-46; Jer. 31:33–35
2. John 16:12, 13
3. Isa. 50:4
4. Matt. 15:13
5. Rom. 10:14

God's part is to draw unto Himself, and to cause the crop to grow.

The seeker who is being drawn will receive God's word when they hear it.

God speaks His word in season to the one who is weary through willing instruments.

Chapter 4
Why Jesus Was Sometimes Silent

Encountering Demons at 30,000 Feet

The elderly woman sitting at Rich Hillman's left side on a flight from Detroit to Indianapolis was greatly agitated.

While the plane was still loading, she frantically blurted out to the attendant, "Can you move me to a seat where I can smoke" (This was in the days when there were a few smoking seats in the back)? She continued, almost in hysterics, "I have to smoke right now. This has been a horrible weekend."

Rich's morning prayer of surrender and petition for witnessing opportunities came to mind. He sent up an additional prayer for wisdom. Her words were an expression of weariness on her part. Not only does she have an addiction, but she is obviously stressed.

In witnessing, timing is essential. The Holy Spirit did not prompt Rich to say, "This is a good time to stop smoking. You know it will kill you." Nor was he compelled to ask if she wanted to study the Bible. Rich found himself focusing on understanding her needs rather than anxiously pursuing his need to witness. He mentioned that, often after the flight gets under way, passengers can move and she could likely transfer to a smoking seat.

Words tumbled from the woman's lips about how she had lost her husband several years earlier. Their son was a wonderful young man, bright and upright. She had struggled to help him through medical school. Right after graduation, he had been killed in a horrible auto accident. Now she had come to visit her sister only to find that her sister was dying. Rich listened sympathetically. The man on his right was also attentive.

She continued, "And when I went to visit Jerusalem, I was walking up the steps to the temple and began to levitate. Why am I telling you this? You will think I am crazy. Oh, why should I care, I'll never see you again anyway. And I have this thing where if a man touches me he gets an electric shock."

She not only had Rich's attention and that of the man on his right, but now the folks in the seat in front turn an ear their way. Rich found himself angry with the enemy for the way he had treated this poor, struggling woman. He prayerfully and respectfully began to speak. "I do not think you are crazy. I am a Seventh-day Adventist Christian and

I believe in the supernatural" (It is good to identify oneself fairly early on in conversational evangelism). The timing was not yet right for a study on spiritualism.

About that time the stewardess came by and said, "Ma'am, we have a smoking seat free now if you would like to change."

"Oh, I am having a wonderful conversation, I want to stay here," she responded.

Rich continued to talk about the reality of the supernatural and what the Bible has to say about angels. The flight was not a long one. Those seated in front seemed as fascinated with the discussion as his seatmates were.

As they neared the end of their flight, she looked out the window and exclaimed, "Are we in Indianapolis already?"

"Yes," the man on the right replied, "and you haven't had to smoke either."

"But what I would really like to know," she hurriedly asked, "what are those beings that come into my room at night?"

There was too little time to give a Bible study on the state of the dead and Rich didn't want to cut her off from further study. The Holy Spirit prompted the words, "Do you know any Seventh-day Adventists?"

"Yes, I am a registered nurse and I worked in the office of a Seventh-day Adventist physician."

Rich assured her that if she would get in touch with that doctor and ask him, he would tell her what those beings are. Then he asked if she would read a book if he sent it to her.

She answered, "I will read anything you send me." She gave him contact information.

When Rich returned home, he found a copy of the colporteur edition of *Bible Readings*. He marked several pages of comforting promises for those who have lost loved ones, including the artist's depiction of fallen angels impersonating loved ones.

At Christmas time, Rich and his wife received a card from the woman with money inside. She said that the book had meant so much to her that she wanted to pay for it.

Have you ever thought that there are times when silence is best in soulwinning? There were occasions when Jesus did not respond to certain questions. He left unsaid some things that might have been said because the people were not ready to receive them. It is not only important to know *what* to say in personal evangelism, but equally as important to know *when* to say it. This sense of timing, like knowing what to say, is the work of the Holy Spirit. For Jesus, it started with a daily baptism of the Holy Spirit.

> From hours spent with God He [Christ] came forth morning by morning, to bring the light of heaven to men. Daily He received a fresh baptism of the Holy Spirit. In the early hours of the new day the Lord awakened Him from his slumbers, and His soul and His lips were anointed with grace, that He might impart to others. His words were given Him fresh from the heavenly courts, words that He might speak in season to the weary and oppressed. "The Lord God hath given Me," He said, "the tongue of the learned, that I should know how to speak a word in season to him that is weary: He wakeneth morning by morning, He wakeneth Mine ear to hear as the learned." Isaiah 50:4. (White, *Christ's Object Lessons*, p. 139)

Four Powerful Secrets of Conversational Evangelism

Isaiah 50:4 contains four powerful secrets of conversational evangelism:

1. The text says, "The Lord God has given me the tongue of the learned…" When we surrender to God for the task of soulwinning, the Holy Spirit prompts our words. This is a direct, creative action on God's part. The Lord told Moses, "I will be with your mouth…and will teach you what you shall do" (Exod. 4:15).

2. Isaiah 50:4 continues, "That I should know how to speak a ***word***…" It is the Word of God that contains converting power. When the seeker asks questions and is receptive, it will be the words of Scripture that will work miracles on the heart.

3. The word is spoken in season. That means that the powerful words of Jesus are spoken at the right time. I believe this is the reason that Jesus was sometimes silent. Timing is everything. We do not plant seeds in the snow. There are times when people are ready and eager to hear and times when they are not. The Holy Spirit will give discernment to know not only the right things to say, but when to say them. Too often, well-meaning witnesses try to force in a word here and there. It is like trying to plant seed on the sidewalk if the listener is not receptive.

> *Timing is everything. We do not plant seeds in the snow. There are times when people are ready and eager to hear and times when they are not.*

Inspiration gives this insight concerning timing when Jesus spoke to the woman at the well:

> This woman was in an appreciative state of mind. She was ready to receive the noblest revelation; for she was interested in the Scriptures, and the Holy Spirit had been preparing her mind to receive more light...Light was already flashing into her mind. The water of life, the spiritual life which Christ gives to every thirsty soul, had begun to spring up in her heart. The Spirit of the Lord was working with her. (White, *The Desire of Ages,* p. 190)

4. Not only are the words and timing given by the Holy Spirit, but He identifies the ones to whom the words are to be spoken—"to him who is weary." This pictures a person who is burdened and has a need. The Holy Spirit will guide the faithful and committed witness to such ones. The sense of oppression surfaces in many ways, but the person who is open to the promptings of the Holy Spirit will be sensitive to discern this weariness in tone of voice or expressions. The following stories illustrate these principles.

Words in Season for the Giant in the Way

The man in the doorway stood six feet, five inches tall. He was built like an NFL defensive end or World Wrestling Association professional. He introduced himself as Jed. The church elder and pastor had prayerfully come to visit a church member who had left her husband and was now living with Jed. They introduced themselves and told him that they were there to visit with Jill. He invited the two in and said that they could talk to him about Jill. The pastor mentioned that they were concerned for the wellbeing of the flock. They were visiting Jill because the church loved her. They explained that love includes treating others in a loving way.

Jed jumped to his feet and shouted, "Do you mean to tell me that the loving thing for Jill to do is to return to her husband when he has been abusive to her?" He heatedly continued, "I am a certified clinical counselor and my professional opinion is that her husband will never change."

It was difficult because the pastor realized that there were legitimate concerns in Jill's relationship with her husband. The Lord certainly did not condone abuse, but this did not make it right for Jill to solve the problem by moving in with another man.

The pastor sent up a prayer for wisdom and found these words escaping his lips: "Jed, have you ever been born again?" The Holy Spirit not only gave these words, but instant understanding as to why they were chosen. If Jed said "Yes," the next comment would be, "Then you know a person can change." If he said "No," the question would be, "How can you say the new birth cannot change a person if you have not experienced it?"

Jed dropped to the couch as though he was shot with a taser. He mumbled, "Well I had some sort of experience but…"

Again, the Holy Spirit brought Scripture to mind. "Jed, what would you do with the Scripture that says, 'Therefore if any man be in Christ, he is a new creature: old things are passed away; behold, all things are become new'?"

Jed began to shake. He went over to a desk and opened a drawer and fumbled around for something. The pastor wondered if he might be going after a gun. He remembered that Jed had told Jill's husband when he had come for her, "I will just take you out in the field and beat you and beat you and leave you to bleed to death."

Still, the Holy Spirit gave strong words that rolled off the pastor's tongue. "Jed, you come across as though you are guilty."

By this time, Jed had found his smoking pipe, but his hands were shaking so hard he could hardly light it. His next words were amazing; "I *am* guilty."

The pastor replied, "The only cure for guilt is Jesus Christ."

Jed said that he and Jill had talked about going to church. He called her and she came out. The pastor explained to her how God loved her and had sent them to talk with her because she was precious in His sight. God wanted what was best for her, her children, and her husband. Things were still in the process of change when the pastor left the district.

I share this experience to illustrate how the Holy Spirit teaches one to say the right thing at the right time. If the pastor had said those things in the stands at a football game, he and the elder might have both fled bleeding and naked like the sons of Sceva did when they were attacked after trying to cast out devils. Sometimes the Spirit prompts comforting words and other times He speaks words that cut through human sophistication.

Weary of Men

Speaking a word in season to the one who is weary is seldom abrasive, however. Jane sat in the chair while her beautician, Marlene, worked on her hair.

"I have had it with men," Marlene said. She knew Jane was a Christian from earlier talks. Marlene told of her failed marriage and how she had just squabbled with the man with whom she was living. She asked, "What is it like in your home?"

Marlene was expressing weariness. Jane told what it is like when both husband and wife love the Lord. Jane shared Christian books with Marlene. On future visits, Jane and Marlene enjoyed talking about their mutual faith in Jesus.

Weary of Cancer

Veronica waited anxiously in the cancer specialist's office. She struck up a conversation with Jessica, a young woman who appeared quite distraught. The women became friends and journeyed through their cancer treatment together. Jessica appreciated the prayers of Veronica and her husband on her behalf. She asked questions and was invited to their home fellowship Bible study group. Jessica accepted Christ and was baptized.

Weary from Fear

Sandy had requested Bible studies after watching Christian television. When the pastor and lay Bible worker visited, Sandy's first question was, "What are all those grasshoppers mentioned in the book of Revelation? I am scared to death. Aren't you frightened?" Sandy was expressing a real spiritual need. She was open to a gospel presentation and accepted Christ enthusiastically.

Weary from Guilt

The man next to Mike in the airplane was easy to talk to. He was a pilot. It was his job to fly above the airport when it was socked in with fog. He salted the clouds so it would rain and clear the skies. He asked what Mike did and learned that Mike was a college teacher and also a pilot. They talked pilot talk. He said he was going to his mother's funeral and added, "If anyone was ready to go it was my mother. That's more than I can say for myself."

The Holy Spirit was talking to him and he was expressing his weariness. That is the time when a gospel presentation can be most meaningful.

Weary of Living without Jesus

There are times when the Holy Spirit will use us to help a person sense their weariness and longing for something better. Scott and Chuck were visiting missing members. It was Friday night when John came to the door with a bottle of beer in his hand. The television was blaring in the background. John had previously served as an elder in the church. Scott and Chuck visited casually for a bit. John had left his wife and given her the nice home. He was living in a small basement apartment with his house cat. Scott could sense that John was lonely. He talked about Jesus and asked John if he would be willing to invite Jesus into his heart.

John said, "I have no desire to."

Scott could feel the presence of the Holy Spirit yearning for John. He prayed for words as he realized that, considering they were of a similar age, he could be like John if not for the grace of God. Tears began to flow down his cheeks as he said, "John, would you be willing to pray for the desire."

"Yes, I can do that."

Scott prayed and John repeated after him, "Please give me the desire to want to invite you into my heart."

John jumped up from his knees and said, "Now I want everything you can give me about Jesus."

They left Bible lessons. Later, John met Scott at work and asked for books, pamphlets, and all he could find about Jesus. He said he wanted to return to church and his wife.

Weary of Staying Home from Church

Archie, like John, had served as a church elder, but then separated from his wife and dropped out of church. He had not attended for fifteen years. Geoff was praying through his network of friends and relatives when Archie came to mind. He remembered that he had watched the Super Bowl with Archie in times past. When he called Archie, he asked what he was doing on Super Bowl Sunday. Archie responded, "I was hoping you would come and watch the big game with me."

Archie lived 360 miles away, but on game day, Geoff was there. Archie turned on the TV and brought out snacks. As they watched the opening kickoff, Archie turned down the TV and said to Geoff, "Do you believe in prayer?"

Geoff shared a number of experiences of answered prayer. Archie said, "I have a sense that someone is praying for me."

Geoff told about his experience in prayer and how Archie had come to mind. They kept the sound down and talked about spiritual things during the entire game. Archie looked pensively away from the TV. His words were full of emotion; "I want to go back to church. I want things to be like they used to be."

Would you like to have greater insight to discern expressions that portray spiritual needs? Would you like to know how to supply that need? Take advantage of all the training you can get. The Lord will use it. Most of all, experience a daily baptism of the Holy Spirit as Jesus did. Future chapters will provide more details and examples of how to do this.

Chapter 5
God Takes the Reins

"Have you read this book?" Burt held out a copy of the *New York Times* best seller, *The Harbinger*, by Rabbi Jonathan Cahn. Rob looked at the book and noted that he saw Cahn via video on Pat Robertson's Internet Christian News Network. Burt admitted, "I don't know the Bible well enough to know whether he is on target or not. You know Bible prophecy. I want you to read it and tell me what you think."

Rob said, "I will order it as soon as I get home from the family reunion. I will read it and we can get together and talk about it."

Burt, being Rob's brother-in-law, is one of the members of Rob's *oikos* (see page 67). Rob and Burt have had several conversations over political concerns. Burt had shared a DVD with Rob and the two had exchanged books on Bible prophecy. Burt had not attended church since leaving academy before graduation, and that was at the invitation of the principal. Rob had always liked Burt. They played golf on occasion, and always seemed to enjoy their time together.

Rob had been praying for Burt for some time with brotherly love. He put himself in Burt's place and felt in his behalf a searching for answers. Burt had recently quit smoking and, on doctor's orders, had given up his occasional beer. Rob shared a copy of Dr. Ben Carson's book, *America the Beautiful*, with Burt. He told Burt that he could share the book with his patriotic friends.

Rob asked for the spirit of discernment to know when to speak a word in season to the one who is weary. Rob is careful not to try to do the work of the Holy Spirit by pushing Burt to be rebaptized and go back to church.

> ***Rob asked for the spirit of discernment to know when to speak a word in season to the one who is weary.***

The key point of *The Harbinger* is that America, like ancient Israel, has been given warning after warning, and unless America turns back to God, our nation is doomed. Burt had listened to Glenn Beck, who is proclaiming a similar message and had recommended *The Harbinger*. At this point, Rob discerned that it was not the time to dispute Cahn's fiction novel approach or his application of prophecy, but rather find the points where Cahn agrees with other Bible prophecies. Rob noted that Cahn is a Messianic Jew and wondered what Cahn thinks of the Seventh-day Sabbath. He checked out websites and video presentations on the Internet. He listened to Cahn's sermon at the prayer breakfast prior to the last presidential inauguration. Cahn sounded like an Old Testament prophet warning America in no uncertain terms with a message of "repent or perish."

Rob sent for the book, as well as the two DVDs on Cahn's presentation concerning Isaiah 9:10 and the current happenings in the United States. He saw this as a possible fulfillment of this promise:

> Let me tell you that the Lord will work in this last work in a manner very much out of the common order of things, and in a way that will be contrary to any human planning...God will use ways and means by which it will be seen that He is taking the reins in His own hands. The workers will be surprised by the simple means that He will use to bring about and perfect His work of righteousness. Those who are accounted good workers will need to draw nigh to God. They will need the divine touch. They will need to drink more deeply and continuously at the fountain of living water, in order that they may discern God's work at every point. (White, *Testimonies to Ministers and Gospel Workers*, p. 299)

Rob again prayed for the spirit of discernment to know what words to speak at this season in Burt's life. Burt and his wife seemed eager to study Bible prophecies. Rob prayed that the Holy Spirit would guide him to point out Bible prophecies that predict national ruin when nations reach the point of national apostasy. In addition, prophetic insight from Ellen G. White that paralleled some of Cahn's conclusions seemed to be appropriate.

While Burt, his wife, family, and friends were keenly focused on turning to the Lord with their whole hearts, it was also crucial that they understand how to accept Jesus as a personal Savior.

Rob and Nancy traveled to visit with Burt and Sue. While watching Jonathan Cahn's video, questions arose about current events and Bible prophecy. Rob opened his Bible and shared texts and explanations that applied to our day.

A man in Burt's Patriot group had mentioned that he had studied into the Seventh-day Adventist religion and found it to be works-oriented. This opened the door for Rob to give his personal testimony concerning righteousness by faith and present the gospel to Burt and Sue.

After their visit, Rob and Nancy continued to pray for Burt and Sue. He remembered that Burt had asked which version of the Bible he thought was best. He had mentioned that he liked the New American Standard Bible, but for the sake of familiarity, the New King James Bible is especially good for studying prophecy.

Since it was close to Burt's birthday, Rob and his wife sent a Bible as a birthday gift. When Burt called to thank them, Rob mentioned that when he had started reading the Bible again, after being away from it for a while, he found the "begats" (genealogies) a little boring. He suggested that Burt follow a pattern of reading some from the Gospel of John, then Genesis and Psalms, Proverbs, and other New Testament books. Rob offered a set of Bible study guides that cover the major points of the Bible. Burt said he would follow his suggestions.

Rob asked Burt if he would be interested in a set of Revelation studies, and the reply was affirmative. He sent the lessons and continued to pray for Burt and his family.

Later, after a golf game, Rob and Burt sat talking. Rob had noticed that Burt did not take his customary chew of tobacco at frustrating points in the golf game. As they talked about world conditions, Burt said, "I think people just don't want to do the right thing." Rob asked him to explain.

"Well, I have always heard that it is harder to quit chewing than it is to stop smoking. Now smoking, that was hard, but some time back I just said to God. 'Help me stop chewing.' That has been over a year and I have not chewed since."

Rob said, "Burt, that is just what we have been talking about. By nature, we can't do the right thing, but when we ask Him, God will come in and take over." Burt's countenance showed more peace than Rob had ever seen on a man's face. He knew that Jesus had found a place in Burt's heart. Burt was unashamed of his tears and Rob was unashamed of his. Burt died from a heart attack several months later. His wife said that he had been starting his day by reading his Bible for some time. Rob was so glad for the power of prayer and the power of the Holy Spirit. He looks forward to eternity where there will be wonderful grounds to roam and chat, better than any country club on this old world.

You too can pray for the Spirit of discernment to notice interest or openness on the part of friends, acquaintances, and family. You can give attention to their concerns and ask the Lord for words to speak in season to the one who is weary. You can feed the spiritually hungry with Christ-centered content, thus guiding them to sources of truth.

Chapter 6
Praying for Other People's Success; Dramatic Answers

Kevin and Bud worked together as literature evangelists. Kevin sold books regularly. It was difficult for Bud to listen to success stories as the two relaxed in the evenings. He became more and more discouraged and talked of quitting. Kevin had the habit of praying as he walked from door to door. He prayed for the people behind the doors and for wisdom to reach them with the gospel. He decided that rather than praying for his own success, he would spend every prayerful moment praying for Bud's success. That evening, Bud was all aglow. He had sold more books than Kevin did. It was a little difficult for Kevin to listen to Bud's glowing stories, but in the depths of his heart he realized that it is more blessed to give than to receive.

Pastor Dasher began seeing dramatic church growth when church members committed to spending at least ten minutes in prayer on a daily basis. Ninety-two new members were baptized in a little over two years. Backsliders and missing members returned to the fold. The church and parking lot were filled to overflowing. They started conducting two services and planted a new church.

Pastor Dasher felt he might be in danger of taking the credit for himself, so one day in prayer, he said, "Lord, help me lead souls to You, and let them join one of the other churches in the area. I want this to be simply for Your sake, not mine."

Pastor Dasher received a phone call soon after that prayer. It was Steven. "Hello Pastor. My wife and I are Rosicrucian (a combination of occultism, Jewish mysticism, and Christian Gnosticism). We are vegetarian. We became vegetarians because we thought it would help our marriage, but rather than help it is causing friction in our home. I called you because I heard that Seventh-day Adventists are vegetarians. I would like to talk to you about how you make a vegetarian lifestyle work in your home."

Pastor Dasher met Steven at the church. After getting acquainted a bit, the pastor asked, "Why did you want to become vegetarian?"

"Because we want to come closer to God," Steven replied.

"In your Rosicrucian belief, what do you do when you make a mistake?"

"We try harder to keep from making that same mistake."

"Do you know what Christians believe about making mistakes?"

"No, what?"

"We believe that no matter how hard we try, we can never be good enough to get close to God, so He came down to be close to us. If your wife were to get upset and say a harsh word against you, you could either retaliate or you could remain silent. If you remain silent, you pay a price in wounded feelings." Steven said that he certainly could understand that analogy.

The pastor continued, "Our sin against God is like that harsh word. If God were to retaliate, we would die, but God chooses to let the sin fall upon himself so that He pays the price. We could not be good enough to reach God, so He came down and became a man in order to reach us. He came to bear our sins against Himself on the cross."

Steven exclaimed, "IS THAT WHAT IT MEANS TO BE A CHRISTIAN?"

Pastor Dasher explained from the Bible the plan of salvation. He asked Steven if he would like to place his sins on the innocent Lamb of God and be completely forgiven.

"Yes!" Steven replied.

They knelt together and Steven repeated a prayer of acceptance after the pastor. "Lord I realize that I am a sinner and need a Savior. I confess my sins and place them upon the innocent Lamb of God. I believe He bears my sins and died in my place. I should have been the one to die. I want Jesus to be Lord of my life. Thank you, God, for salvation."

When they rose from their prayer, Steven said, "Now I want to study to the depths to know for sure that what you have told me is true. I want you to load me with every book that I need. I am going away to my cabin and will not come out till I know for sure."

Several months passed. Steven again called the pastor. He said, "I have read everything you gave me. It is all true. My wife has also read them. We have been attending the Seventh-day Adventist Church nearest to our home. We plan to be baptized there this coming Sabbath."

Pastor Dasher had mixed emotions. He was glad for Steven and his family, but he also would have liked to add them to his list of baptisms for the year. Then he remembered his prayer.

When Pastor Dasher left the district, Steven came to visit. He said, "Pastor, I heard you were leaving. I just want you to know that it was because of you that I accepted Jesus as my Savior and have become a Seventh-day Adventist. My wife and I are so happy. I plan to go into the literature evangelism work. If you had not shared the gospel of salvation with me, I would never have known the Savior." Pastor knew in his heart that this was the kind of success that he really wanted.

I believe these stories underscore a principle in praying for the success of other people. It is one of the greatest arguments against Satan's claims that God has no right to answer our prayers because we are all selfish.

I believe this is why the Bible encourages group prayer. "Again I say to you that if two of you agree on earth concerning anything that they ask, it will be done for them by My Father in heaven" (Matt. 18:19). This is why I believe it is good, when a person makes a personal request in prayer, for others to say "Amen" and/or add a prayer of agreement. Some of the most dramatic answers to prayer have been witnessed by this author because I prayed, in my own private devotions, for the requests of others.

It would be well for those in a class or prayer group to remember other class members by name in prayer and uplift the special concerns of those for whom they are praying. It would be more difficult for the enemy to claim that it is a selfish prayer. Consequently, I believe it adds power to our prayers.

When we pray in the name of Jesus, it means that we pray for others as He would pray for them. When you pray for souls, ask the Holy Spirit to intercede through you with the unselfish purposes that God has in mind for that person. This helps us to focus on the needs of others more than our own.

When visiting missing members, it is more important to first listen to their stories before offering help. As you listen, be aware of spiritual pain and hunger. Those who are easily hurt may have sensitivities associated with past relationships. Emotional pain often transfers to a sense of rejection by God. Ask the Lord to give insight into their needs and help bring comfort and assurance. Not only are missing members often lonely for friendship, but most of all they have a deep need to be at one with God.

Pastors Phillips and Johns visited missing members Claude and Vivian. It was Friday evening and Claude was watching a secular television program. After friendly conversation, Pastor Phillips asked how things were going spiritually. Claude recounted how years ago his son had been involved with the pastor's son in a sporting accident, and the pastor's son was killed. He said that he always felt that the pastor held it against him; and he felt condemned by God. He could not feel comfortable at church. The pastors led Claude and Vivian through a gospel presentation, affirming the love, mercy, and acceptance of Jesus.

The next Sabbath, Claude and Vivian were in church, eagerly volunteering to serve in whatever way they could be of use. They remained faithful until they fell asleep in the Lord. They were joyous and happy people rejoicing in their Savior's love. We never know what burdens people might be carrying.

1. John 6:44-46; Jer. 31:33–35
2. John 16:12
3. Isa. 50:4

One who is weary

Listen for weariness

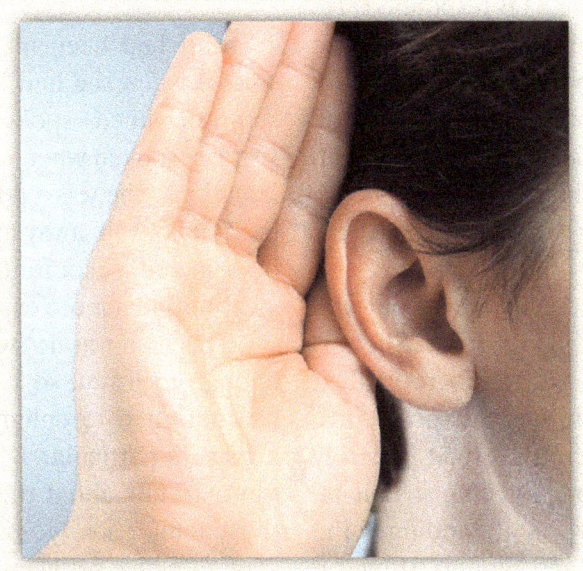

Missing members have a story.

Chapter 7
Work with Interested People

He was carrying a fishing pole, so I excitedly told him about the hundreds of fish that I saw from the bridge.

"Those fish are not biting," he responded. He went on to explain, "You can fish all day and cast a line right in front of a school of fish and they will not touch the bait if they are not hungry. Then all of a sudden, when the fish decide it is time to eat, they will bite on almost anything."

It is important to fish for souls when and where the "fish are biting."

Kari was young and innocent, yet devout and desirous of being used by the Holy Spirit. She was absent as the other young people regrouped at the street corner. One of the students pointed to a porch down the street where she stood patiently listening. She had been there for almost half an hour. As I approached, I saw a man standing in the doorway. He was red-faced and ranting. If ever a man were emotionally engaged, it was this man. With animated gestures, he loudly explained how the beatitudes were all included in the design of the ancient Egyptian pyramids.

It is important to fish for souls when and where the "fish are biting."

Kari had been making contacts to find Bible studies when she had knocked on the door of this self-proclaimed spokesman for God. She had scarcely spoken when he began his "inspired" proclamations. She was a polite person. She felt it would be rude to walk away and thought perhaps he must be a sincere seeker for truth. Her partner had pulled away to find a more experienced worker to assist.

This man was not willing to stop his raging long enough to listen, so I kindly led Kari away while he continued to enlighten the neighborhood and no one in particular. This presented a good opportunity to talk about the most common pitfalls that the enemy uses to entice faithful workers away from effective soulwinning. It can be a trap for the witness to become a captive audience for those who are pushing their own views, or to spend time with those who are willing to talk for hours about trivia, or to enter into debate with those who may be attacking our faith. It is enticing because it may seem like the witness is engaged in sharing the gospel, when in reality they may simply be detained from finding real interests.

Jesus taught His disciples to work with interested people and not try to convince those who were unresponsive. He told them that when people were not receptive, to "shake the dust off your feet" (Matthew 10:14) and go on. He also said, "No one can come to Me unless the Father who sent Me draws him; and I will raise him up at the last day" (John 6:44). The next verse continues, "It is written in the prophets, 'And they shall all be taught by God.' Therefore everyone who has heard and learned from the Father comes to Me" (v. 45).

People who have willingly heard the voice of the Holy Spirit will want to learn of the Father. They will be open to receiving truth that will continue to bring them closer to God.

It is the first work of the effective soulwinner to find those who are being drawn by the Holy Spirit. Jesus asked His disciples to watch for interested listeners, seek them out, and give first attention to those with a receptive mind. The disciples "watched for interested hearers, explained the Scriptures to them, and in various ways worked for their spiritual benefit" (White, *The Desire of Ages*, p. 349). "On this first tour the disciples were to go only where Jesus had been before them, and had made friends" (p. 351).

There are ministries that seek to awaken interest. I am not saying we should not engage in these. However, the Holy Spirit will help us find truly interested seekers at smoking cessation clinics, cooking schools, health education seminars, small groups, community service events, and the like.

Even in the process of studying the Bible with willing people, the Christian worker must protect against being drawn off into irrelevant issues that have little to do with essential doctrine. We should seek to spend our time with those who respond to simple truth. "Search the Scriptures with those who are willing to be taught" (White, *Evangelism*, p. 458). "Do not stop to try to convert the one who is speaking words of reproach against your work" (White, *Gospel Workers*, p. 359).

> Plain, pointed arguments, standing out as mileposts, will do more toward convincing minds generally than will a large array of arguments which cover a great deal of ground, but which none but investigating minds will have interest to follow…Our success will be in reaching common minds. (White, *Testimonies*, Vol. 3, p. 39)

Some who in Paul's day listened to the truth, raised questions of no vital importance, presenting the ideas and opinions of men, and seeking to divert the mind of the teacher from the great truths of the gospel, to the discussion of non-essential theories and the settlement of unimportant disputes. Paul knew that the laborer for God must be wise enough to see the design of the enemy, and refuse to be misled or diverted. The conversion of souls must be the burden of his work; he must preach the word of God, but avoid controversy. (White, *Gospel Workers*, pp. 311–2)

Chapter 8
Word in Season Opportunities

Nick decided to try his hand at construction at the age of seventy-two. He applied for a job with a masonry company and was on the job at 7:00 a.m. with a number of other workers who had responded to the ad on Craigslist. It took a bit of effort to catch on to new techniques and get up to speed after forty years of being away from commercial brick work. Stan was assigned as Nick's partner. Nick had been hired onsite without showing the boss what he could do. It soon became apparent that Stan had more recent experience, and the lead which had been assigned to Nick was transferred to Stan without any formal agreement.

Nick noticed that Stan was patient in dealing with his slower ways. He picked up the slack when Nick didn't quite keep up. Nick prayed for an opportunity to speak a word in season. A young coworker came up to them and told a dirty joke. Nick looked at him kindly, but did not laugh. Stan didn't laugh either. When there was a little break in the action, Nick went over to Stan and said, "Let me introduce myself. I am a retired minister."

Stan replied, "I knew you were."

"What! Are you a prophet?"

"No, I have just been around ministers and could tell."

As the day wore on, Stan and Nick continued to chat about working conditions and pay scale for the laboring man. Stan said something that shocked Nick. "If I were to die tonight, there is not a soul in the world that would care."

Nick was taken aback, yet didn't want to reply with silence. "Your dog would care."

"Well, maybe for a little while."

"Stan, you are a really good guy. You could be cussing me out for being so slow, yet you came over and did some of my work. You are the kind of person that heaven is made for."

"Well, I've tried church, but felt out of place. The preacher pointed me out and said, 'Now even if you dress like this man, you are important to God.' I didn't like being pointed out. My work clothes were all I had to wear."

Nick talked more about Jesus with Stan and they agreed to get together in the future sometime.

On another occasion, Nick was working with a

similar partner who was also fast and helpful, but struggling with his Christian experience.

He asked Nick, "What do you do if you know what is right but don't feel like doing it?"

Nick responded, "Don't try to change your feelings, but confess them and ask for the mind of Christ."

"But what if you don't feel like asking for the mind of Christ?"

"Confess that also."

These are examples of how a word can be spoken in season on the job. See Chapter 30 for more illustrations. Note the following quotes:

Jesus Speaks a Word in Season

His *messages of mercy* were varied to *suit His audience*. He knew "how to speak a word in season to him that is weary" (Isaiah 50:4); for *grace* was poured upon His lips, that He might convey to men in the most *attractive way the treasures of truth*. He had *tact* to meet the prejudiced minds, and *surprise them with illustrations that won their attention*. Through the imagination He reached the heart. His illustrations were taken from the things of daily life, and although they were simple, they had in them a wonderful depth of meaning. The birds of the air, the lilies of the field, the seed, the shepherd and the sheep,—with these objects Christ illustrated immortal truth; and ever afterward, when His hearers chanced to see these things of nature, they recalled His words. Christ's illustrations constantly repeated His lessons. (White, *The Desire of Ages*, p. 254, emphases mine)

Word in Season to Those within Our Sphere of Influence

The earnestness of our efforts for others should be in proportion to the value of that which God has given to us to present to the world. All who keep in a *prayerful frame of mind*, looking to God for *heavenly wisdom*, will be able, through the *grace of Christ*, to speak a word in season to those who are brought within the *sphere of their influence*. (White, *Gospel Workers*, p. 224, emphases mine)

Every day that passes brings us nearer the end. Does it bring us also near to God? Are we watching unto prayer? Those with whom we associate day by day need our help, our guidance. They may be in such a condition of mind that a word in season will be sent home by the Holy Spirit as a nail in a sure place. Tomorrow some of these souls may be where we can never reach them again. What is our influence over these fellow travelers? What effort do we make to win them to Christ? (White, *Counsels for the Church*, p. 67)

Were they alive to the interest of the work, they would see souls close by their side to whom they could speak a word in season, of *warning, encouragement, or comfort*. There are tempted, tried souls all about us for whose ruin Satan is much more interested than are the professed brethren of Christ for their salvation. But it is the work of the servant of Christ to sow beside all waters, and the promise is, that "he that goeth forth and weepeth, bearing precious seed, shall doubtless come again with rejoicing, bringing his sheaves with him." (White, RH June 16, 1896, par. 11, emphases mine)

Word in Season on the Job

The workers in our sanitariums are continually exposed to temptation. They are brought in contact with unbelievers, and those who are not sound in the faith will be harmed by the contact. But those who are abiding in Christ will meet unbelievers as He met them, refusing to be drawn from their allegiance, but always ready to speak a word in season, always ready to sow the seeds of truth. They will watch unto prayer, firmly maintaining their integrity, and daily showing the consistency of their religion. The influence of such workers is a blessing to many. By a well-ordered life they draw souls to the cross. A true Christian constantly acknowledges Christ. He is always cheerful, always ready to speak words of hope and comfort to the suffering (White, *Counsels on Health*, pp. 252–3).

Suffering Ones

All around us are afflicted souls. Here and there, everywhere, we may find them. Let us search out these suffering ones and speak a word in season to comfort their hearts. Let us ever be channels through which shall flow the refreshing waters of compassion. (White, *Lift Him Up*, p. 95)

If you have tasted that the Lord is gracious, if you know his saving power, you can no more keep from telling this to some one else than you can keep the wind from blowing. You will have a word in season for him that is weary. You will guide the feet of the straying back to the fold. Your efforts to help others will be untiring, because God's Spirit is working in you. (White, RH November 24, 1904, Art. A, par. 16)

Chapter 9
Cooperating with Angels

My trainee was a student from a nearby Christian high school. There, faculty and students had spent several days studying about and praying for the baptism of the Holy Spirit. It was 106 degrees. We were glad for the shade the small porch provided as we rang the door bell. A well-dressed woman in her early sixties opened the door.

"Hi, we are telling folks about a new Christian TV station in your town." We handed her a brochure for the 3ABN translator, which highlighted programming and station numbers.

She exclaimed, "Do you mean to tell me that there is a free Christian TV station right here in this town? I am paying thirty-five dollars a month for Christian TV."

We handed her the first community Bible reading lesson. "Along with this, we are encouraging folks to participate in a summer Bible reading program."

She accepted the lesson with enthusiasm. The next eight people who answered the door gave similar responses.

At our tenth house, a man answered the door and said, "We don't watch anything but a special cable network."

As we walked to the next house, I spoke encouragingly to my trainee. "I have never seen people so responsive. This must be the outpouring of the Holy Spirit. Nine out of ten people have been receptive. The interesting thing of it is that about every fortieth home we find someone crying and praying for light."

We rang the next doorbell. No one came so we rang again. A young woman appeared. We handed her the brochure with the same message about 3ABN telecasts.

She said, "I was raised a Catholic but I married a Seventh-day Adventist. A woman from the Seventh-day Adventist Church studied the Bible with me and I attended the Adventist Church for a while, but somehow I didn't seem to fit in."

It was obvious that she was a true seeker. I replied, "We will leave the first lesson with you today and one of the women from the church will come by next week, review this lesson with you, and give you another."

"Which church?"

I was sure she would recognize Seventh-day Adventist programming, so I said, "Oh, the one right here in _____" (I've decided not to mention the location).

"Yes, but what denomination?"

"Seventh-day Adventist."

She burst into loud crying. Through her sobs she testified, "When you rang the bell, I was on my knees praying and crying for direction to know which way to turn. I didn't answer the door right away because I had to go into the bathroom to dry my eyes."

All three of us stood weeping with the realization that angels had worked in her preparation of heart and our arrival at her house. I believe we can expect more and more angel guidance as we come close to the end of time.

> When they are willing to count all things but loss that they may win Christ, their eyes will be opened to see things as they really are. Then they will turn away from the earthly attractions to the heavenly. Then they will see the true nature of the worldly, selfish enjoyments that they now value so highly, and these things that they now hold so dear will be given up.
>
> All heaven is looking upon you who claim to believe the most sacred truth ever committed to mortals. Angels are waiting with longing desire to cooperate with you in working for the salvation of souls. Will you refuse this heavenly alliance in order to maintain your connection with society where God is not honored, where His commandments are trampled upon? (White, *Selected Messages*, Book 2, p. 136)

> If you walk humbly with God you may unite with the students not of our faith, agreeing with them as far as possible by dwelling upon points wherein you harmonize. Make no effort to create an issue. Let them do that part of the work themselves. Let them see that you are not egotistical, pharisaical, thinking no one loves God but yourselves, but draw them to Christ, thus drawing them to the truth. All heaven is engaged in this work. Angels wait for the cooperation of men in drawing souls to Christ. "We are laborers together with God." (White, *Manuscript Releases*, Vol. 4, p. 49)

> The angels can not take our places; but they stand ready to co-operate with us in drawing souls to Christ; and they are soliciting us to work in fellowship with them. (White, *The Signs of the Times*, December 10, 1896, par. 13)

> God calls for consecrated men, who are willing to deny self. The work of the heavenly intelligences is constant and earnest; for they are intent upon drawing men to Jesus. This is the manner in which ministers should labor. Their message should be, "Whosoever will, let him take the water of life freely." In the ministration of angels, they do not labor so as to shut any soul out, but rather to gather them all in; but if the message of the gospel is to go to all men, human agents must co-operate with the angel workers. Divine and human agencies must combine in order to accomplish the great work of saving the souls of the lost. Man cannot work out his own salvation without divine aid, and God will not save him without willing, decided co-operation. Human agencies must be educated; they must be sufficient for this great work, and their growth and education depend upon their union with divine forces. God provides all the capabilities, all the talents, by which men may enter the work; but the highest development of the worker for God can never be attained without divine co-operation. (White, *The Review and Herald*, August 30, 1892, par. 4)

> From the case of Cornelius we may learn a lesson that we would do well to understand. The God of heaven sends His messengers to this earth to set in operation a train of circumstances which

will bring Peter into connection with Cornelius, that Cornelius may learn the truth. Through angel ministration Peter is brought into cooperation with the inquiring souls who have all things in readiness to hear the truth and receive advanced light... (White, *Evangelism*, p. 558)

Chapter 10
God Uses Those Who Recognize Their Need

If you are like so many of God's true believers, you have wished that God could use you more effectively in soulwinning. You may feel inadequate in this regard as one of the least of His saints. If so, you are closer to the solution than you might think. God often uses humble people to accomplish great things. The utmost requisite for receiving power to witness is the recognition of our great need of the Holy Spirit.

The chosen twelve were not from the elite class of scholars or clerics. Some, like the sons of thunder (James and John), would probably fight at the drop of a hat. One was of the profession suspected of fraudulent dealings against his own countrymen. They may not have always been perfect in appearance. Most must have come home smelling like fish. One of them openly denied Christ with cursing and swearing, yet God used him to convert thousands. The Holy Spirit worked through all of them to turn the world upside down. The power to witness came when they received the baptism of the Holy Spirit.

You may be tempted to tell yourself that you could never be a true disciple. This is faulty thinking. If God could use the apostles, with all their faults and weaknesses, surely He can use anyone dedicated to Him. You may not consider yourself to be perfect, but I would guess that you have never lopped off a man's ear with a sword as did one of the most effective evangelists recorded in the Bible. In order for God to fill vessels of clay, they must first be empty. A major first step in receiving an infilling of the Holy Spirit is to become aware of this emptiness. This is part of the reason it took the disciples ten days of heart searching before Pentecost. It was essential for them to know their need.

> *If you are like so many of God's true believers, you have wished that God could use you more effectively in soulwinning. You may feel inadequate in this regard as one of the least of His saints. If so, you are closer to the solution than you might think.*

Before honor is humility. To fill a high place before men, Heaven chooses the worker who, like John the Baptist, takes a lowly place before God. The most childlike disciple is the most efficient in labor for God. The heavenly intelligences can co-operate with him who is seeking, not to exalt self, but to save souls. (White, *The Desire of Ages*, p. 436)

The disciples felt their spiritual need and cried to the Lord for the holy unction that was to fit them for the work of soul saving. (White, *The Acts of the Apostles*, p. 37)

Those only who are constantly receiving fresh supplies of grace will have power proportionate to their daily need and their ability to use that power. Instead of looking forward to some future time when, through a special endowment of spiritual power, they will receive a miraculous fitting up for soul winning, they are yielding themselves daily to God, that He may make them vessels meet for His use. Daily they are improving the opportunities for service that lie within their reach. Daily they are witnessing for the Master wherever they may be, whether in some humble sphere of labor in the home, or in a public field of usefulness. (White, *Ye Shall Receive Power*, p. 153)

The Spirit furnishes the strength that sustains striving, wrestling souls in every emergency, amidst the hatred of the world, and the realization of their own failures and mistakes. In sorrow and affliction, when the outlook seems dark and the future perplexing, and we feel helpless and alone,--these are the times when, in answer to the prayer of faith, the Holy Spirit brings comfort to the heart. (White, *The Acts of the Apostles*, p. 51)

In the first chapter, Carl recognized his need. He felt guilt and shame for his failure to reach souls for Christ. His son listened to him pour out his heart with expressions of guilt. He led his parents through a gospel presentation. An understanding of the gospel and assurance of salvation provides the first step in receiving the baptism of the Holy Spirit, for the baptism affirms assurance and brings more of the joys of salvation than ever before. Then he suggested that they start by making friends with neighbors and praying for them.

Some time later, the son again came for a visit. His mother pointed out the window of their home and said, "Do you see that woman walking down the street. She lives upstairs. We have become good friends. We invited her to attend evangelistic meetings. She was baptized and now attends church with us."

God uses humble people. If you feel your need for power and insight in soulwinning, then praise the Lord for the prompting of the Holy Spirit and follow on to know the Lord.

Chapter 11
Ask for the Baptism of the Holy Spirit

Some may wonder why we need to pray for the Holy Spirit, since a) He is already at work in our lives and b) God will send the latter rain when He is ready. Ron Clouzet, former director of North American Division Evangelism Institute at Andrews University SDA Theological Seminary, wrote a book (*Adventism's Greatest Need,* 2011) on the baptism of the Holy Spirit. He addresses this question. The title of the book itself proclaims the urgency of our need to ask for the Holy Spirit.

Clouzet mentions that Ellen G. White stated in 1897 that the people of that time were "now" living in the time of the latter rain (p. 179). The entire quote which Clouzet referenced is as follows:

> "Ask ye of the Lord rain in the time of the latter rain." Do not rest satisfied that in the ordinary course of the season, rain will fall. Ask for it. The growth and perfection of the seed rests not with husbandman. God alone can ripen the harvest. But man's co-operation is required. God's work for us demands the action of our mind, the exercise of our faith. We must seek his favors with the whole heart if the showers of grace are to come to us. We should improve every opportunity of placing ourselves in the channel of blessing. Christ has said, "Where two or three are gathered together in my name, there am I in the midst." The convocations of the church, as in camp-meetings, the assemblies of the home church, and all occasions where there is personal labor for souls, are God's appointed opportunities for giving the early and the latter rain. (White, *The Review and* Herald, March 2, 1897, par. 6)

The circumstances may seem to be favorable for a rich outpouring of the showers of grace. But God himself must command the rain to fall. Therefore we should not be remiss in supplication. We are not to trust to the ordinary working of providence. We must pray that God will unseal the fountain of the water of life. And we must ourselves receive of the living water. Let us, with contrite hearts, pray most earnestly that *now, in the time of the latter rain,* the showers of grace may fall upon us. (White, *The Review and* Herald, March 2, 1897, par. 7)

Dr. Clouzet writes:

Many Adventists simply assume that because the 'early rain' was given at the time of Pentecost, and the latter rain at the end time, that there is a vast vacuum of the Spirit in the intervening centuries. They conclude that the Spirit is not with God's people today, although it would be more accurate to say that God's people are not with the Spirit today. They see God as holding back His Spirit and that He must be worked on and persuaded to release the Spirit. The thought suggests that the spiritual shortcomings of God's people today are because they have not received the outpouring of the 'latter rain'. Insidiously, the blame is shifted to God, and we sit back waiting for him to take the initiative in correcting things by pouring out the 'latter rain' of the Spirit. (Clouzet, *Adventism's Greatest Need*, p. 183)

Now we know that no cosmic alignment, no political liaisons, no ecumenical developments are delaying the outpouring of the latter rain. What is delaying the latter rain at the *time* of the latter rain – a time that has lasted over a century to date – is simply the church's unwillingness to surrender all. That is, the members' lives must be watered by the early rain before the latter rain will do its work. (Clouzet, *Adventism's Greatest Need*, p. 182)

He further quotes Ellen White from the following source:

We are not willing enough to trouble the Lord with our petitions, and to ask Him for the gift of the Holy Spirit. The Lord wants us to trouble Him in this matter. He wants us to press our petitions to the throne. The converting power of God needs to be felt throughout our ranks.

(White, *Fundamentals of Christian Education*, pp. 537–8)

This means that we can now experience the fulfillment of God's promises concerning the outpouring of the Holy Spirit as on the day of Pentecost. We can ask as did the disciples. We can expect greater working of the Spirit in the lives of our friends and loved ones. A whole vista of opportunity lies ahead. We can experience this blessing anew as we review the promises given to the disciples prior to Pentecost.

When Jesus appeared to His disciples after His resurrection, He told them that they would be baptized by the Holy Spirit not many days in the future (see Acts 1:5). He taught them to ask for the Holy Spirit and believe that God is ready to send Him even more than an earthly father is eager to give good gifts to his children (see Luke 11:13). The prophet Zechariah admonishes, "Ask the Lord for rain in the time of the latter rain" (Zech. 10:1). Mrs. White says, "The outpouring of the Holy Spirit on the day of Pentecost was the former rain, but the latter rain will be more abundant. The Spirit awaits our demand and reception" (*Christ's Object Lessons*, p. 121).

This asking should be with confidence as though it is already an accomplished fact. Jesus said, "Therefore I say to you, all things for which you pray and ask, believe that you have received them, and they will be *granted* you" (Mark 11:24, NASB).

Our faith is strengthened by claiming promises. During their ten days of prayer for the Holy Spirit, the disciples claimed the promise that Jesus had given. They focused their faith on His work of intercession. They knew that they were unworthy, yet Jesus had won the victory over Satan and the right to grant a special outpouring of the Holy Spirit. He promised, "I will ask the Father, and He will give you another Helper, that He may be with you forever" (John 14:16, NASB).

He said, "Truly, truly, I say to you, if you ask the Father for anything in My name, He will give it to you. Until now you have asked for nothing in

My name; ask and you will receive, so that your joy may be made full" (John 16:23, 24, NASB). Prophetic insight opens our eyes to the activity of the disciples as they prayed for the fulfillment of the promise:

> They knew that they had a Representative in heaven, an Advocate at the throne of God. In solemn awe they bowed in prayer, repeating the assurance, "Whatsoever ye shall ask the Father in My name, He will give it you. Hitherto have ye asked nothing in My name: ask, and ye shall receive, that your joy may be full." John 16:23, 24. Higher and still higher they extended the hand of faith, with the mighty argument, "It is Christ that died, yea rather, that is risen again, who is even at the right hand of God, who also maketh intercession for us." Romans 8:34. (White, *The Acts of the Apostles*, pp. 35–6)

Lost in wonder, the apostles exclaimed, "Herein is love." They grasped the imparted gift (White, *The Acts of the Apostles*, p. 38).

It is not likely that we will have occasion to assemble for ten days as did the disciples, but we can spend at least ten minutes a day praying and claiming promises for the outpouring of the Holy Spirit upon us and those within our spheres of influence. Recognizing our need of the Holy Spirit and asking for this outpouring in our lives are two beginning steps in experiencing a present-day Pentecost.

Chapter 12
Experiencing God's Presence

The honest seeker who prays for the outpouring of the Holy Spirit into his/her life can expect to experience fulfillment of the promises of Jesus concerning the coming of The Comforter. He told his disciples, "I will not leave you orphans; I will come to you" (John 14:18). Not only will Jesus visit the petitioner, but the Father will manifest Himself as well. "Jesus answered and said to him, 'If anyone loves Me, he will keep My word; and My Father will love him, and We will come to him and make Our home with him'" (v. 23).

Jesus further stated, "But when the Helper comes, whom I shall send to you from the Father, the Spirit of truth who proceeds from the Father, He will testify of Me" (15:26). When claiming these promises, the supplicant will meditate on the matchless character and unselfish ministry of Jesus.

> He who feels most deeply his need of divine aid will plead for it; and the Holy Spirit will give unto him glimpses of Jesus that will strengthen and uplift the soul. From communion with Christ he will go forth to work for those who are perishing in their sins. He is anointed for his mission; and he succeeds where many of the learned and intellectually wise would fail. (White, *The Desire of Ages*, p. 436)

Meditating on the life of Jesus is not a wearisome task. Rather, it is a joyous drinking at the fountain of blessing. It does require some effort, however, to make time in our busy schedule for quiet reflection. The rewards of spending time with Jesus far outweigh the effort it takes to set aside time for personal devotions.

As you read the accounts of the interactions between Jesus and other people, try putting yourself in each story. For example, imagine yourself as the Samaritan woman traveling to the village well. You walk alone to escape the ridicule and shame that would come from the normal gathering of

> *The rewards of spending time with Jesus far outweigh the effort it takes to set aside time for personal devotions.*

peers. You recognize the emptiness in your life as you try to avoid the subject when Jesus inquires into the secrets of your personal conduct. Notice how kindly He treats you. You feel like he reads your heart, yet relates to you as a friend. This awakens hope and you long to know how you stand with God. You have heard of the coming Messiah. You mention this. Jesus looks at you with perfect peace, love, and acceptance. "I who speak to you am *He*" (4:26). Your heart is thrilled by the fact that God has made Himself known to you and shown more mercy than you could ever have imagined.

Remembering His offer to give you living water, your soul is filled with a power never before experienced. In your haste to share the good news, you leave your water pot for the moment and make the mundane duties of life second priority. You can't wait to share the gospel with those who need it most.

> When you have received the baptism of the Holy Spirit, then you will understand more of the joys of salvation than you have known all your life hitherto. "Ye shall receive power, after that the Holy Ghost is come upon you; and ye shall be witnesses to Me…unto the uttermost parts of the earth." (White, *Manuscript Releases*, Vol. 5, p. 231)

Mrs. White highlighted a noteworthy phenomenon as the disciples prayed for the Holy Spirit in the upper room. "Like a procession, scene after scene of His [Jesus'] wonderful life passed before them. As they meditated upon His pure, holy life they felt that no toil would be too hard, no sacrifice too great, if only they could bear witness in their lives to the loveliness of Christ's character" (*Acts of the Apostles*, p. 36).

As the petitioner allows the Holy Spirit to search his/her heart and human weaknesses are revealed, He brings a fresh vision of the cross. Zechariah 12:10 will become a reality—"And I will pour on the house of David and on the inhabitants of Jerusalem the Spirit of grace and supplication; then they will look on Me whom they pierced. Yes, they will mourn for Him as one mourns for *his* only *son,* and grieve for Him as one grieves for a firstborn."

The hunger and thirst for righteousness is satisfied by eating the flesh and drinking the blood of the Son of God. The seeker realizes that the only way a perfect sinner can get together with a perfect God is through a perfect Savior who is able to "save to the uttermost those who come to God through Him, since He always lives to make intercession for them" (Hebrews 7:25).

Chapter 13
Cautions Regarding the Baptism of the Holy Spirit

Speaking in Tongues
Because of false teaching in this area, it is important to mention that a baptism of the Holy Spirit is not equated with speaking in unknown tongues. Jesus received a baptism of the Holy Spirit at the Jordan River and on a daily basis, yet we have no record that He spoke in tongues other than His known languages (see chapters 14 and 28).

Taking the Name of the Holy Spirit in Vain
For every true gift, there are many counterfeits. Some claim a connection to God that gives direction when they may be simply following their own thoughts and/or desires. Others misapply statements identifying the Holy Spirit as the only power that can bring about conversion, so they sit back and do nothing to win souls. They expect the Holy Spirit to do it all. There are others who claim to have received the Holy Spirit when their lifestyles testify to slothfulness, self-indulgence, and careless living.

Seeking an Emotional High
Though the fruit of the Spirit includes love, joy, peace, the presence of Christ, and all other blessings in its train, Holy Spirit baptism does not consist of working ourselves up to an ecstatic state. The baptism of the Holy Spirit is for the purpose of witnessing, rather than rapture.

Gifts of the Spirit are Active
The gifts of the Holy Spirit, including miraculous powers, are manifested in the act of witnessing. We claim the promises and receive assurance, but the power comes when we employ the gifts committed to Christ in ministry.

NONE SHOULD WAIT IN IDLE EXPECTANCY FOR THE BAPTISIM OF THE HOLY SPIRIT. THE SPIRIT OF GOD IS GIVEN FOR SERVICE. AS CHURCH-MEMBERS GO FORTH AT GOD'S BIDDING, THE HOLY SPIRIT COMES TO GIVE EFFICIENCY AND POWER.
(White, *Pamphlets*, No. 120, p. 16)

Holy Spirit Is Not Given for Selfish Purposes

Simon Magus received a stern rebuke for trying to obtain the Holy Spirit for personal gain and to bolster his reputation as one who was considered "the great power of God" (Acts 8:9–20). Some may attempt to use their experience with the Holy Spirit to coerce others to their way of thinking or force them into carrying out their wishes. We have this inspired counsel:

> We cannot use the Holy Spirit. The Spirit is to use us. Through the Spirit God works in His people "to will and to do of His good pleasure." Philippians 2:13. But many will not submit to this. They want to manage themselves. (White, *The Desire of Ages*, p. 672)

> God has poured his Spirit upon his servants, and qualified them to use their ability and talent in revealing truth to those who sit in darkness; but the very ability God has given by which to reveal truth to others, men, perverting their talents, employ to deceive; for they use their gifts as did Satan when he deceived the angels of heaven, and exalt self, causing their God-given abilities to administer to their own glory. (White, *The Review and Herald*, October 23, 1894, par. 6)

Clinging to Sinful Thoughts and Practices

> Christ has promised the gift of the Holy Spirit to His church, and the promise belongs to us as much as to the first disciples. But like every other promise, it is given on conditions. There are many who believe and profess to claim the Lord's promise; they talk *about* Christ and *about* the Holy Spirit, yet receive no benefit. They do not surrender the soul to be guided and controlled by the divine agencies. (White, *The Desire of Ages*, p. 672)

Making Surrender a Meritorious Work

It is essential to be willing to surrender every sinful attitude, thought, and practice in order to receive the Holy Spirit. Yet this is the point where many fail. If we could be saved simply by surrender alone, we would not need a Savior. The devil may try to get us to find within ourselves some meritorious quality of surrender that recommends ourselves to God. Surrendering is not making ourselves feel surrendered, but a choice to ask God to take over our lives. We make this choice by the exercise of faith.

> No outward observances can take the place of simple faith and entire renunciation of self. But no man can empty himself of self. We can only consent for Christ to accomplish the work. Then the language of the soul will be, Lord, take my heart; for I cannot give it. It is Thy property. Keep it pure, for I cannot keep it for Thee. Save me in spite of myself, my weak, unchristlike self. Mold me, fashion me, raise me into a pure and holy atmosphere, where the rich current of Thy love can flow through my soul. (White, *Christ's Object Lessons*, p. 159)

Looking Within for Evidence of the Baptism of the Holy Spirit

Though we must remain constantly surrendered by faith to Christ, there is a danger that the enemy will try to keep us looking within to produce this condition. When we confess wrong thoughts, feelings, and desires, and ask for the mind of Christ, there is most often an instantaneous relief and infilling of the Spirit.

> *Though we must remain constantly surrendered by faith to Christ, there is a danger that the enemy will try to keep us looking within to produce this condition.*

However, the enemy will try to convince us that we would never have wrong feelings if we have truly received a baptism of the Holy Spirit. He will try to get those inclined toward self-righteousness to form an elite holiness club and reign in all to their standard of piety. This can be a trap. Notice the following statement:

> There are toils and conflicts, self-denials and secret heart trials, for us all to meet and bear. There will be sorrow and tears for our sins; there will be constant struggles and watchings, mingled with remorse and shame because of our deficiencies. (White, *Testimonies for the Church*, Vol. 3, p. 187)

Chapter 14
Spared by the Spirit from Unknown Tongues

"Have you experienced the baptism of the Holy Spirit?" Mrs. Schmidt asked as she looked inquisitively into Pastor Dalton's eyes. He knew she was really asking whether he had spoken in tongues. The enemy has touted a counterfeit baptism of the Holy Spirit for so long that many sincere Christians mistakenly associate the term with speaking in tongues. The Seventh-day Adventist pastor would not answer that part of her question until later.

He flashed a big smile and replied, "Yes, I have experienced the baptism of the Holy Spirit. Praise God!"

Mrs. Schmidt was a rather large woman. Her face had expressed warmth and kindness. Now her look was that of amazement and surprise.

Dr. Warner, a dentist, was a member of the men's witnessing group in the church. He had followed a lead for Bible studies, reviewed several lessons with Mrs. Schmidt, and called and asked if the pastor would conduct the next Bible study with her. He said that she was attempting to get him to speak in tongues while he was trying to convince her about the importance of the Ten Commandments and the Sabbath.

Pastor Dalton knew that he must explain the issue from the Bible. He was confident that the Lord would give answers because He has promised wisdom. The pastor had spent time in study and prayer, confessed and forsaken all known sin, and claimed God's promises—"Go and I will go with you" and "I will put words in your mouth."

Mrs. Schmidt continued to fish for affirmation that he had spoken in tongues. "What did the Holy Spirit do when He came to you?"

The pastor sent up a quick silent prayer and asked the Lord for Scripture, then replied, "Just what he promised He would do in John 16:8." They turned to the text together and Mrs. Schmidt read, "And when He has come, He will convict the world of sin, and of righteousness, and of judgment." The pastor went on to read 1 John 3:4. "Whoever commits sin also commits lawlessness, and sin is lawlessness." This was not exactly what she wanted to hear.

Then they opened to John 15:26. "But when the Helper comes, whom I shall send to you from the Father, the Spirit of truth who proceeds from the Father, He will testify of Me." Pastor Dalton gave his testimony of how he had been praying outdoors and experienced a sense of God's perfection and righteousness as manifested in Jesus and the Ten Commandments. The more he contemplated the perfect purity and righteousness of Jesus, the more selfish and sinful he seemed to be in his own eyes. He went on to speak of the Jesus revealed in Scripture. He talked about His eternal power and glory, loving kindness, mercy, compassion, sacrifice for sins, and embodiment of the law of self-sacrificing love. He explained how he had been overwhelmed with a sense of the perfect love of God.

Pastor Dalton told how the passage in John 16:9–11 had been fulfilled in personal experience; how the Holy Spirit had brought many shortcomings to his mind and convinced of the greatest sin of all—unbelief. In his dialogue with God, he realized how cruel it is to not believe God. He told how he confessed his unbelief as a sin. He shared how the Holy Spirit lifted his eyes to Jesus as Intercessor and convinced him that "because the ruler of this world is judged", he was free from all condemnation in Christ. He talked with passion about the meaning of the cross and the joy of experiencing the presence of Jesus. He testified that he saw God as a perfect God and himself as a perfect sinner, but Jesus as a perfect Savior, able to save to the uttermost those who come to God by Him.

Pastor Dalton did not tell Mrs. Schmidt his entire experience, but he remembered how, after renewing his reception of Jesus as a perfect Savior, he thought, *'It is as though God says of me for His sake, "This is my beloved son in whom I am well pleased."'* The thought seemed too wonderful and almost blasphemous until he went into the house and opened the book *The Desire of Ages*. There he found the following quote:

> And the word that was spoken to Jesus at the Jordan, "This is My beloved Son, in whom I am well pleased," embraces humanity. God spoke to Jesus as our representative. With all our sins and weaknesses, we are not cast aside as worthless. "He hath made us accepted in the Beloved." Ephesians 1:6. The glory that rested upon Christ is a pledge of the love of God for us. It tells us of the power of prayer,--how the human voice may reach the ear of God, and our petitions find acceptance in the courts of heaven. By sin, earth was cut off from heaven, and alienated from its communion; but Jesus has connected it again with the sphere of glory. His love has encircled man, and reached the highest heaven. The light which fell from the open portals upon the head of our Saviour will fall upon us as we pray for help to resist temptation. The voice which spoke to Jesus says to every believing soul, This is My beloved child, in whom I am well pleased. (White, p. 113)

Mrs. Schmidt listened attentively, then said, "But didn't you just want to open your mouth in praises when the Holy Spirit came?"

Again, Pastor Dalton breathed a silent prayer and replied, "Oh yes, I often praise Him and sometimes sing His praises, but I do this just like it says in Scripture: 'I will pray with the spirit, and I will also pray with the understanding. I will sing with the spirit, and I will also sing with the understanding'" (1 Cor. 14:15).

Mrs. Schmidt looked annoyed and loudly inquired, "Don't you speak in tongues?"

Again, he asked the Lord for wisdom. The Spirit brought to mind that Jesus received a baptism of the Holy Spirit after His water baptism, but He had not spoken in unknown tongues. "Oh no, I do not speak in tongues," he said. "Speaking in tongues is one of the gifts of the Spirit, but Jesus received a baptism of the Holy Spirit and Scripture does not say that He spoke in tongues."

Mrs. Schmidt put on a loud preacher voice and said, "You Adventists! If you would stop preaching dry old doctrine and start speaking in tongues you would do so much more good than you are now doing!"

Pastor Dalton silently prayed, *'Lord give me one more text.'* His eye fell on a text and the Holy Spirit revealed it in a light that he never before saw.

There it was clear and bold: "Now, brethren, if I come unto you speaking with tongues, what shall I profit you, except I shall speak to you either by revelation, or by knowledge, or by prophesying, or by doctrine" (1 Cor. 14:6, KJV)? He put his finger on the text, put the Bible in front of Mrs. Schmidt, and asked her to read it.

She read and said, "Yes but…"

He then asked her to read it again. She did so and was very quiet. He prayed that she would continue to reflect on God's Word and evaluate her experience on the basis of what the Holy Spirit had revealed.

> *The voice which spoke to Jesus says to every believing soul, This is My beloved child, in whom I am well pleased.*

A daily baptism of the Holy Spirit was the secret for the power that Jesus manifested in winning souls. It was from this daily baptism that He received words to speak in season to the weary ones. As a people, we need to understand more of this truth. The Holy Spirit's name has been taken in vain by some. This, along with the enemy's work, has limited an understanding of the power available through the Holy Spirit. There is a growing awareness, however, of this beautiful truth in the church.

Holy Spirit baptism does not separate one from the realities of life. It does not turn one into a somber, formalistic saint. The Holy Spirit does not depart from us when we put our hands in mud and grease, nor does the baptism of the Holy Spirit take away our zest for life or sense of humor. It does not cloister us from practical living. We are told that the latter rain will bring every other blessing in its train. The baptism of the Holy Spirit brings righteousness by faith, Christian experience, prayer ministry, joyous living, and gospel outreach to higher and more satisfying levels.

For further study on the baptism of the Holy Spirit, see chapters 23–28.

Chapter 15
The Gifts of the Spirit in Operation

The essential baptism of the Holy Spirit is a deepening daily experience. Prayer, Bible study, and meditation result in focusing on the cross and amazing work of salvation accomplished in our behalf by Jesus.

A daily imbibing of the Spirit naturally flows into practical action. The gifts of the Spirit are given to equip the believer for ministry. Gifts such as teaching, healing, helps, administration, leadership, hospitality, and others all play a part in growing the body of Christ (see Eph. 4:7–16). All the gifts of the Spirit are given for the purpose of ministry. Not all have the gift of evangelism; but when the gifts are active in a church or small group, the combined effect will be evangelism and growth.

Praying Church Experience
Pastor Barlow encouraged his church members to set aside ten minutes a day for prayer. The gifts of the Spirit were manifested among the believers. The pastor involved the members by inviting them to join with him in ministry. He affirmed various gifts of the Spirit when discerned in his members by means of prayer and observation.

Pastor Barlow saw that there were some dedicated members who were naturally outgoing, friendly, and comfortable to be around. He affirmed in them the gift of hospitality and gave them a few pointers on how to make visitors feel welcome and comfortable without being overwhelmed. Together they designed guest cards and set up a calendar so that various members with the gift of hospitality could plan to invite guests home for dinner on certain Sabbaths. Greeters engaged guests in conversation by introducing themselves, asking if they knew their way around the building, and taking them to a Sabbath School class (most often the pastor's class, which was designed to prepare people for baptism and ground new members in truth). Greeters learned how to glean information about the guests from their conversation without being invasive. The greeters then gave the filled-out guest cards, along with other information, to the pastor following church.

One of the pastor's spiritual gifts was evangelism, so he invited teams of men and women with this gift to accompany him on evangelistic visits. He trained them how to meet people in a friendly way without pressuring them. He taught them how to depend on the Holy Spirit and work with those who were interested. He demonstrated how to share one's testimony and give Bible studies. The pastor took teams on Tuesday morning from 10:00 a.m. to noon, then additional teams on Tuesday evening from 7:00 to 9:00 p.m. After giving a gospel presentation to those visited, team members followed through with Bible studies. The pastor occasionally accompanied the team during the Bible study. When the prospective church members signed a Bible study guide or response card after a sermon requesting baptism, the pastor visited, reviewed doctrine, and prepared the candidates. Teams first visited those who signed the guest register or response cards from church. The following experience is typical.

One Tuesday morning, the pastor and visitation team arrived at the home of a woman who had signed the guest register. Ronda came to the door. She recognized the pastor and welcomed the team inside. Her husband Cliff was at work. Ronda mentioned that she had been raised a Seventh-day Adventist. She had drifted away, studied astrology, and walked the way of the world for a time. Her cousin Sarah had visited and invited her to attend church with her. The pastor gave a brief testimony and asked Ronda if Jesus were to come today, or if she were to die tonight, would she be sure where she would spend eternity. She said that she would not be sure, so the pastor gave her a gospel presentation and invited her to pray the prayer of reception. She did so and said that she would like to have the team visit her husband and share the gospel with him.

Pastor Barlow and the team visited Cliff, who worked as a meat cutter. He was athletic and muscular. His uncle was a boxer and taught Cliff to fight. He became a boxer and street fighter and rode motorcycles with the Hell's Angels at one time in his life. The pastor gave him a gospel presentation and he also accepted Christ. The women from the team studied with Ronda and Cliff and they were baptized into fellowship with God's people.

Here is an example of how other spiritual gifts were manifested. A godly woman came to the pastor and said that she would like to see the church sponsor a health seminar conducted by a team from Loma Linda. As she described the program, Pastor Barlow affirmed her gift of healing and asked how much the seminar would cost. She estimated that it would cost $400. He encouraged her to talk to the financial administrator of the church, a man with business education and experience. He thought to himself that this man would be able to tell her we didn't have the money. However, she came back, excitedly telling that he gave permission and said that they could come up with the money. The pastor attended planning sessions for the health seminar, but it was entirely planned and conducted by lay members who were enthused about ministry in their gifted area. The seminar was a tremendous success. This created awareness in the community and was part of a holistic approach to evangelism.

The pastor felt a great relief and was energized to continue training lay Bible workers. There were many details of church operation that required the attention of the church board. He affirmed the gift of administration in his head elder and left leadership of the board with him while he trained disciples in personal evangelism. The pastor divided leadership roles into groups of five, each with five groups under them. The head elder had five elders under his leadership. Each of the elders had a specific responsibility such as visitation, youth, worship, etc. The head deacon had deacons under his leadership, also with specific responsibilities, like being in charge of building maintenance, community services, church services, etc.

When people were called by a member of the nominating committee to serve in a particular position, their gifts were affirmed and a job description was read. For example, "Marcia, it is clear to us that you have an artist's touch for floral arrangement and that you are dedicated to serving the Lord. We would like to ask you to be in charge of providing flowers for the church and for funerals, weddings, Mothers' Day, new arrivals, and for those in the hospital. You will work under Florence the head deaconess and can name those you would like to have work with you. You will have a budget of [whatever amount] for the year."

The church of 400 members grew in attendance. They went to two church services to accommodate room for seating and cars in the parking lot. In a period of a little over two years, a number of former members returned to the fold and ninety new members were baptized. One volunteer lay Bible minister was instrumental in preparing thirteen people for baptism in one year. Several members partnered with members from a neighboring church and planted an additional church.

Chapter 16
Soul Winning through Spiritual Gifts

The promise of the Spirit is not appreciated as it should be. Its fulfillment is not realized as it might be. It is the absence of the Spirit that makes the gospel ministry so powerless. Learning, talents, eloquence, every natural or acquired endowment, may be possessed; but without the presence of the Spirit of God, no heart will be touched, no sinner be won to Christ. On the other hand, if they are connected with Christ, if the gifts of the Spirit are theirs, the poorest and most ignorant of His disciples will have a power that will tell upon hearts. God makes them the channel for the outworking of the highest influence in the universe (White, *Christ's Object Lessons*, p. 328).

This quote speaks of learning, talents, eloquence, every natural or acquired endowment being empowered by the Holy Spirit and becoming a channel for God to work. Gift placement instruments and spiritual gift inventories may help one to have insight into effective ministry. There are many possibilities for ministry in each gift. Most of God's people have a combination of gifts. For example, a person with the gift of music may minister in a powerful way. If that same person also has the gift of leadership and/or teaching, he/she can lead others to use their musical ability for Jesus and teach them how to do so. If these gifts are dedicated to the Lord and empowered by the Holy Spirit, their overall influence will lead others to Christ. The spiritually-gifted person will find ways to give a living and sometimes verbal testimony of God's love. The following possible ministry opportunities may be empowered through common spiritual gifts.

> *If these gifts are dedicated to the Lord and empowered by the Holy Spirit, their overall influence will lead others to Christ.*

Gift of Maintenance

- Conduct free classes for the community on topics like *Tips for Saving Money on Cars, Computers Made Simple,* and *Do It Yourself Household Repair and Maintenance.*

- Include your testimony in your class.
- Partner with those with gifts of mercy, evangelism, etc.
- Form friendships with those who attend class and look for opportunities to speak a word in season.
- Form a group to do free maintenance projects in the community for those lacking skills in this area.
- Give your testimony while working with others or donating your time to others.
- Train young people in maintenance and give your testimony at the appropriate time.
- Remember those within your own household and *oikos*.
- Develop friendships and invite friends to home fellowship groups, SS classes, and evangelistic meetings.

Gift of Mercy or Nurture

- Pray for and visit those who are infirm or invalids. Speak words of encouragement. Read Scripture and pray with them. Loan them inspirational music CDs, Scripture or other inspirational media.
- Cooperate with home fellowship and healing groups by bestowing thoughtful words and deeds of kindness within the group and your *oikos*.
- Minister to those in SS class, small groups, or community classes through warmth, understanding, listening, and words of sympathy.
- Send cards, letters, emails, and/or flowers to those who are mourning, ill, suffering, isolated, or in the military.
- Send cards to newlyweds, families with new babies, etc. from notices in the newspaper.
- Cultivate friendships within your *oikos*.
- Pray for opportunities to speak a word in season to the weary.
- Be ready to give your testimony when the Holy Spirit indicates the time and place.
- Develop friendships and invite friends to home fellowship groups, SS class, and evangelistic meetings.

Gift of Hospitality

- Serve as a greeter, helping guests feel at home without investigating them.
- Invite guests home to share a meal.
- Serve as a host or hostess for a home fellowship Bible study group.
- Serve as a greeter for free community classes in maintenance, health, healing, etc.
- Learn the art of conversational evangelism.
- Serve at various socials.
- Make sure guests at church, SS class, and community meetings feel at home.
- Serve as a greeter for evangelistic meetings.
- Walk in the foyer, looking for guests. Get acquainted with them and invite them to class and/or home for a meal.
- Help with church fellowship meals. Facilitate arrangements for guests.
- Mingle with guests at concerts and other events.
- Help guests sign the guest book, engage in friendly conversation, and share information with the visitation team.

Gift of Healing

- Professional healing professions, including therapists and health educators
- Hospital visitation and prayer for the sick
- Behavior science healing therapy
- Addiction recovery
- Divorce recovery
- Grief recovery
- Healing center group therapy
- Men's ministries
- Women's ministries
- Biblical counseling
- Home visitation, natural remedies, and hydrotherapy
- Have a prayerful spirit as you minister to physical needs

Gift of Teaching

- Facilitating class discussion
- Helping others to think new thoughts and become involved in new actions
- Modeling Christian behavior
- Teaching in children's divisions and Pathfinders
- Conducting classes in healthful living or other practical lifestyle aspects for the community
- Writing teaching materials and Bible studies
- Working with correspondence students on the computer or through regular mail
- Mentoring or discipling on a one-on-one basis

Gift of Leadership

- Anyone who has people who look up to them as an example and/or who have an interest in following or learning from them is a leader.
- A leader demonstrates competency and earns respect
- Helps others realize their full potential
- Motivates others
- Facilitates cooperation and unified action within a group
- Disciples individuals and/or groups
- Mentors others in the Christian walk

Gift of Administration

- Has the ability to manage information and material
- Gives attention to detail
- Communicates well
- Has the ability to organize and keep operations running smoothly
- Fits all the various parts of organizations into a harmonious whole
- Extends the power of various gifts by bringing them together for a unified goal
- Can help others with time management or household management

Gift of Financial Management

- Classes for the community regarding financial management and investments
- Classes for the elderly about financial retirement issues
- Management of funds for ministries

- Financial counseling for those with limited income
- Management of funds to keep organizations operating smoothly

Gift of Evangelism
- Conducts public evangelistic meetings
- Gives Bible studies
- Shares at a home fellowship small group
- One-on-one friendship evangelism
- Child evangelism

Gift of Helps
- Work behind the scenes to assist in any of the ministries mentioned
- Support operation of gifts with finances

Gift of Music
- Leading music in worship
- Writing Scripture songs
- Conducting concerts
- Outdoor concerts, e.g. band, choral, or vocal; invite community
- Singing and playing instruments for worship and evangelistic meetings
- Leading music for SS class
- Sharing your testimony with students

Other examples:

Graphic Arts and Computer
- Design advertising brochures, letters, billboards, and fliers
- Set up a website offering Bible studies or studies in health, finances, etc.
- Set up a blog for interested people
- Cooperate with those with other gifts, e.g. evangelism, healing, and teaching to utilize their skills on a website
- Teach classes in the community for basic computer operation
- Volunteer to assist folks in their homes who are learning how to use a computer
- Set up a learning website for soulwinners, including spiritual gifts inventories

WHOA! Who has time for all this?

As possibilities for ministry continue to surface, one might think, '*I can see lots of things that I might do, but life is already so crowded that all my energy is more than spent.*'

Blocks of Time

One of the best ways to manage is to set aside a block of time during the week. Start with two hours per week. Dedicate this block of time to the most effective means of ministry available. The target goal will be to find an interested person who will be receptive to receiving Bible studies. To begin, you may dedicate most of that time to prayer, preparing through study, making friendly contacts, and sowing seeds within your *oikos*. The time will come when you will find one or more individuals with whom to study the Bible.

If evangelism is not one of your spiritual gifts, you might partner with one who has the gift of evangelism. For example, if you have the gift of hospitality, consider hosting a small group Bible Study led by those with gifts of teaching and evangelism.

Blocking out time can be very liberating. Otherwise there is a tendency to constantly be thinking that everything hangs overhead undone. This can be very wearisome. When you block out time and actually do the most effective thing available, it energizes one to accomplish additional, normal tasks with greater freedom (See Supplement 6, Spiritual Gifts Inventory).

Chapter 17
Holy Spirit and Joy

Joy in the Holy Spirit

The reception of the Holy Spirit is associated with joy throughout Scripture. "And the disciples were filled with joy and with the Holy Spirit" (Acts 13:52). "[F]or the kingdom of God is not eating and drinking, but righteousness and peace and joy in the Holy Spirit" (Rom. 14:17). "Now may the God of hope fill you with all joy and peace in believing, that you may abound in hope by the power of the Holy Spirit" (15:13). "And you became followers of us and of the Lord, having received the word in much affliction, with joy of the Holy Spirit" (1 Thess. 1:6).

> With deep interest and grateful, wondering joy the brethren listened to Paul's words. By faith they grasped the wonderful truth of Christ's atoning sacrifice and received Him as their Redeemer. They were then baptized in the name of Jesus, and as Paul "laid his hands upon them," they received also the baptism of the Holy Spirit, by which they were enabled to speak the languages of other nations and to prophesy. Thus they were qualified to labor as missionaries in Ephesus and its vicinity and also to go forth to proclaim the gospel in Asia Minor. (White, *The Acts of the Apostles*, p. 283)

> As the instruction of Jesus to the apostles was drawing to a close, and as the hour of his separation from them approached, he directed their minds more definitely to the work of the Spirit of God in fitting them for their mission. Through the medium of a familiar intercourse, he illuminated their minds to understand the sublime truths which they were to reveal to the world. But their work was not to be entered upon till they should know of a surety, by the baptism of the Holy Ghost, that they were connected with Heaven. They were promised new courage and joy from the heavenly illumination they should then experience, and which would enable them to comprehend the depth and breadth and fullness of God's love. (White, *The Spirit of Prophecy*, Vol. 3, p. 240)

When you have received the baptism of the Holy Spirit, then you will understand more of the joys of salvation than you have known all your life hitherto. "Ye shall receive power, after that the Holy Ghost is come upon you; and ye shall be witnesses to Me...unto the uttermost parts of the earth." (White, *Manuscript Releases*, Vol. 5, p. 231)

If the Joy is Missing

- Trying too hard to believe?

- Looking for joy as an end in itself rather than a byproduct?

- Failure to ask for the latter rain?

- Failure to let the Holy Spirit search your heart?

- Failure to surrender by faith?

- Dwelling too much on revealed sins?

- Expecting the gifts of the Spirit apart from ministry?

- Ignoring the Holy Spirit?

How to Fix it

- Instead of trying to feel faith, claim His promises and thank Him for hearing you.

- Look at revealed sins only long enough to confess and ask for the mind of Christ.

- Delight yourself in the Lord by meditating on His character and revelation of love in nature.

- Embrace trials as God's way of removing dross and bringing the gold to the surface.

- Remember that an ounce of trial endured for His sake results in tons of blessings and rewards.

- Be willing to lay everything on the altar.

- Confess your lack of faith.

- Rejoice and praise God for sins forgiven, the perfect intercession of Jesus, and the promises to answer your prayers for the lost.

- Rejoice in singing and keep a song in your heart.

- Rejoice in fellowship with other disciples.

- Set your affection on things above rather than on things of earth.

- Find His Word to be a delicious meal and daily bread for the hungry soul.

- Live in expectation of fulfilled promises.

Chapter 18
When No One Seems Interested

Dottie Given had a strong conviction that she should witness for Jesus; but how could she find anyone interested in Bible study? She had small children at home, so she felt that she should not commit to spending time seeking Bible studies with the Bible worker. She asked God for wisdom to know what to do and people with whom she could study the Bible.

The following week, relatives visited. Her cousin Mike had recently married. Marsha, Mike's new wife, found Dottie and her husband Clyde's Seventh-day Adventist lifestyle strange and somewhat undesirable. Mike and Marsha had planned to stay only one night. However, their car unexpectedly needed repairs. They had to wait four weeks for the necessary part. Marsha craved her meat-based diet and was not drawn to the Givens' vegetarian food. Dottie worried that Marsha would be bored and distracted without her normal TV programs. She was concerned about cooking and wondered how they would spend their time. She prayed earnestly for wisdom and soon found games they could all play. Mike and Marsha realized that they enjoyed their time in the Given home.

Since there was no TV and they had no vehicle for transportation, Mike and Marsha went to church with Dottie and Clyde on Sabbath. She was impressed with the way Dottie taught the children. She said, "You know, I like the way your church provides a mothers' room for babies. I think our church is wrong, but don't preach at me."

After they returned home, Dottie and Clyde received a letter from Marsha. She said that she had gone to her priest and asked him questions. He was not able to provide biblical answers. She and Mike were open to Bible study and eventually followed Jesus into membership at Clyde and Dottie's church. Dottie realized that since she could not go out to find interested people, the Lord had sent them to her.

God was not done bringing people to Dottie and Clyde. A man named Jerry came to do electrical work in their home. He found it strange that Dottie and Clyde did not have a television. He noticed that there were never odors of meat cooking when Dottie prepared meals. He asked why they did not eat meat or have a TV.

Dottie responded, "If you would like to know more, we have Bible studies that explain. Would you like to study the Bible?"

Jerry and his wife Ruth accepted Bible studies. They sometimes came up with hard questions. If Dottie and Clyde didn't know the answer, they admitted it and promised to study and find answers. They went to camp meeting and upon their return, they discovered that Jerry and Ruth attended the local Seventh-day Adventist church expecting to surprise Clyde and Dottie, but had not found them. The four of them became close friends. They went to a recreational camp in Idaho and enjoyed water skiing. They often called on Sabbath evenings to get together for popcorn. When the question of jewelry came up, Dottie and Clyde studied the Bible texts with them and told them that they should pray about it and follow their convictions. They removed their jewelry, continued to study, attended church, and were baptized.

After their baptism, Jerry and Ruth moved to southern Idaho and looked for a Seventh-day Adventist church. With none in vicinity, they began studies with others in their home. The fellowship group grew and eventually became a Seventh-day Adventist church. Jerry and Ruth's two girls were in their teens when they had studied with Dottie and Clyde. They were not particularly interested in the studies, so their parents did not push them, but the words they heard as they listened in the background were not without effect.

One of the girls later had medical complications and remembered her mom's religion. Dottie and Clyde prayed with her and she recovered. The girl was assigned to Dottie for physical therapy. They bonded as she helped her learn to walk with artificial limbs. She jokingly called Dottie her "physical terrorist." Dottie said, "Your next assignment is to walk to church."

She did walk to church and she and a number of relatives were later baptized. All this came from the contact with an electrician.

After her children were grown, Dottie and her friend Charlotte went door-to-door with the personal ministries leader from the conference office. They found a number of people willing to participate in a summer Bible reading program. Wanda wrote responses to the lessons and met with Dottie and Charlotte each week for review. The lessons whetted her appetite for more studies, so they took Wanda through additional studies. They grew to become good friends and spiritual partners. Wanda was eventually baptized and joined the church. She corresponded with her son in Alaska. Much to her delight and the delight of her son, she found that he too had been studying the Bible and was baptized into the Seventh-day Adventist Church! What a wonderful fellowship they shared in the way God led in their lives.

The pastor of the church where Clyde, Dottie, and Charlotte were members accepted another call and moved away. The church was without a pastor for nearly a year. When the new pastor arrived, they told him that they had seventeen people ready for baptism. The pastor could hardly believe his ears. He met each candidate, reviewed doctrine with them, and agreed that they were indeed ready for baptism.

Pray for people with whom to study, and be ready for action.

Plant and Tend Seeds in Season Within Your Oikos

The graphic on the right illustrates effective evangelism. The miracle working power of life is in the gospel seed, not in the sower. The sower scatters the seed in fertile receptive soil.

The planter prepares soil by deeds of lovingkindness. He/she may find soil that has been prepared by others—for example, through television ministries, public evangelistic meetings, friends or family of church members, etc. The gospel worker receives a daily baptism of the Holy Spirit and, in the process of praying through his/her *oikos*, asks for a spirit of discernment to recognize fertile soil or plants that are beginning to sprout. He/she asks for wisdom to know how to speak a word in season

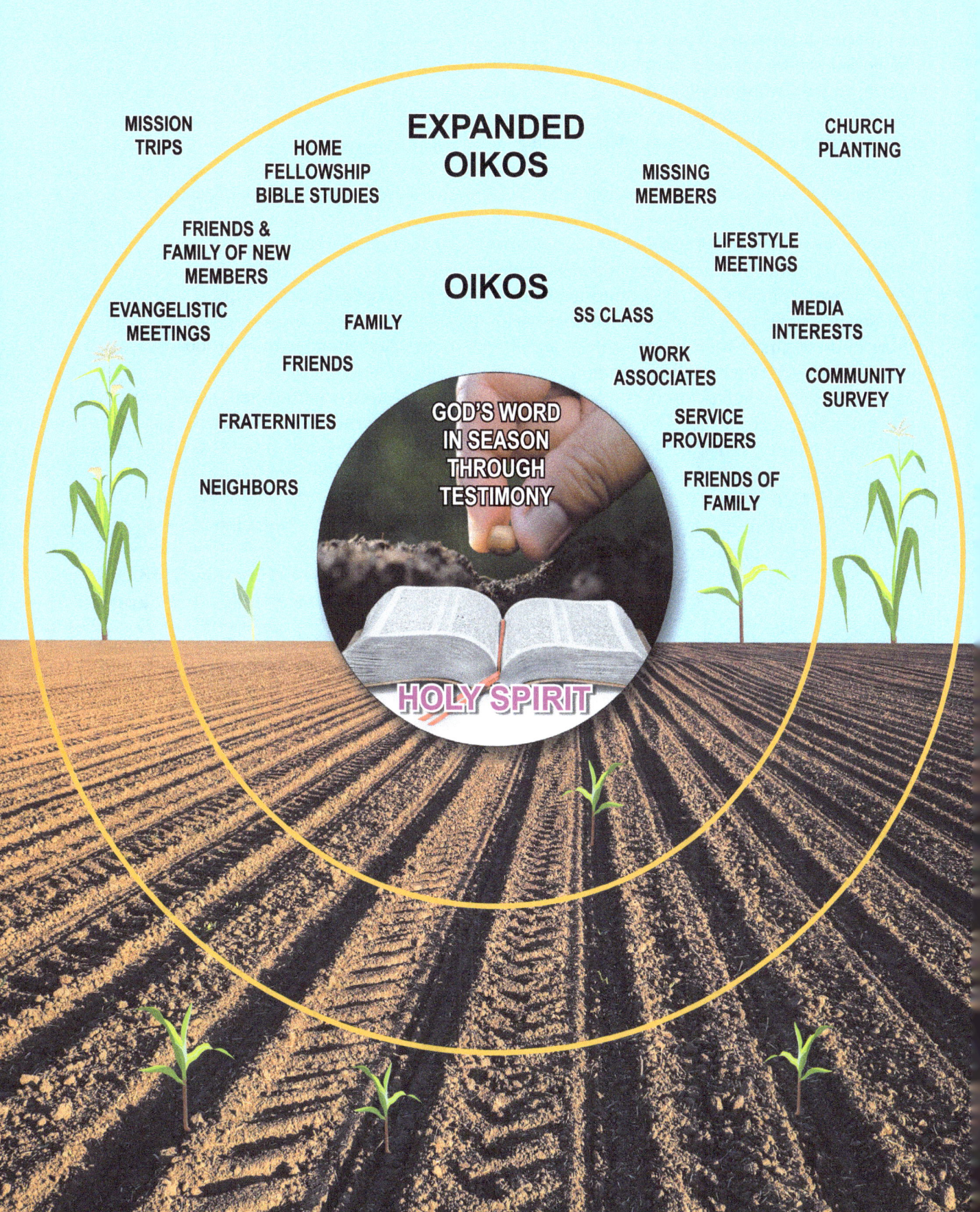

to the one who is weary. When wisdom is revealed, the gospel worker makes a prayer commitment to speak the right words at the right time. The disciple maker targets Bible studies, small group study, evangelistic meetings, or other means of placing the seed.

There are those within the close circle of family, friends, neighbors, acquaintances, and fraternities that may show signs of the work of the Holy Spirit in their lives. Often this may come by way of problems or expressions of interest in spiritual things. The sower focuses primary attention on those who show interest, first within his/her immediate circle, then expands to others that may show spiritual awakening by responding to offers for Bible studies, calls at evangelistic meetings, etc. The ground becomes a ministry target field of souls in various stages of growth, progressing toward harvest.

The most effective means of sowing the seed is through personal testimony and gospel presentation. The gospel worker feeds the sprouting plants with the nourishment of God's Word and waters with prayer.

There may be several sprouting plants in various levels of one's *oikos*. The worker continues to focus on receptive soil and growing plants, all the while prayerfully looking for new fertile ground or sprouting plants.

When the time is right, the grower puts in the sickle for harvest.

> **The most effective means of sowing the seed is through personal testimony and gospel presentation.**

Finding Those Being Drawn by the Holy Spirit

Jesus sent His disciples first to those with whom He had made friends. There are various ways to follow that example:

1. *Oikos* relationships
2. Recreational evangelism
3. Visitors to church
4. Interested family members and friends of church members
5. Former members
6. Fishing pools
   a. Home fellowship Bible studies
   b. Lifestyle seminars
   c. Grief recovery groups
   d. Addiction recovery groups
   e. Ministry to the blind, needy, invalid, ill, imprisoned
7. Those being drawn by the Holy Spirit through media evangelism
   a. Signs of the Times interests
   b. TV interests—He's Alive TV, 3ABN, Hope Channel; Life-talk Radio as well
   c. Bibleinfo.com
   d. Mailed invitations for Bible studies
   e. Ads in news media
8. Cooperate with others who are throwing out the net
   a. Follow-up evangelistic meetings
   b. Angel seminar, prophecy seminar, Revelation seminar
   c. Follow-up exhibits, e.g. Journey to the Cross, Sanctuary exhibit
   d. Go with a Bible worker to find interests
   e. Go with experienced disciples to find and give Bible studies

f. Short-term mission trips

9. Door-to-door

   a. Use known entities, e.g. He's Alive, SDA billboards

   b. Surveys

Chapter 19
Using the Right Tools

You are about to read more amazing stories of God's miracle-working power in soulwinning. At this point, the enemy may try to make you think that you could never experience such astonishing things. He may urge you to contrast them with your failures, human limitations, and frustrated attempts at witnessing. He may try to present this as evidence that God cannot use you. However, the opposite is true. These stories are reported to encourage you, the reader, to expect the Holy Spirit to work in spite of human weaknesses in a most challenging, hostile environment. Almost every experience reported took place amidst fear, trepidation, foreboding, and seemingly impossible circumstances like those that are common today.

These stories are also selected from a lifetime of experience representing a rather broad field of service. On the other hand, some of the greatest miracles are those that take place in our closest relationships when loved ones turn to Christ with little drama or excitement. Hopefully you can identify with some stories and see ways for the Lord to use you in His service in spite of the difficult times that surround us.

> *These stories are reported to encourage you, the reader, to expect the Holy Spirit to work in spite of human weaknesses in a most challenging, hostile environment.*

Opera Star Sees Mysterious Light

Loretta (not her real name) was a diva opera star who sang in many cities throughout the world. She was raised Catholic, but through the years became involved in the New Age movement. Her daughter Deana became acquainted with a Christian young man. The young man's father, Andy, claimed the promise of the Holy Spirit. As he prayed through his circle of influence, he remembered that when Deana was visiting, she said that her mother enjoyed watching Christian TV programs. He made a prayer commitment to mention Christian videos to her next time she was in the home.

Soon Andy found himself reminded of his prayer commitment as Deana prepared to leave after a visit. Andy was a bit reluctant to mention anything, thinking that the timing was not right to bring up the Bible, but he remembered his prayer commitment, so he asked her if she thought her mother might be interested in seeing some Christian videos.

Deana said, "Yes!" She took the videos to her mother. Loretta invited her friends to watch the videos. They all enjoyed them and wanted copies for themselves. She sent the videos back to Andy, who sent the next lessons in the series.

After number seven, it was time to give a gospel presentation, so Andy called Loretta to see how things were going with the videos. She was enthusiastic; then he asked if she came to the point where she experienced the assurance of eternal life. Loretta began to tell her story.

A crisis had come up in her life and she felt a deep spiritual need. She was involved in interpreting dreams in the New Age movement.

One night she had a vivid dream that would change her life. She saw herself on a cruise ship, which she interpreted as life's journey. The passengers were playing hide and seek and she was "it." She understood this to mean that she was desperately seeking for light like a child trying to find those in hiding. In her dream, she wandered through the long corridors of the ship, feeling lost and alone. She did not know to whom to pray since there were so many channels in the New Age Movement. Then, with her Catholic background, she prayed to Jesus. She called out for guidance. When she looked up in her dream, she saw a blazing light at the end of a corridor. She moved toward the light and saw that it was Jesus. He spoke to her and said, "I am the Way, the Truth, and the Life. No man comes to the Father but by me."

She was shocked awake with the realization that the New Age concept of many channels was in error and knew that she must start reading the Bible to find everything Jesus had to say.

It was soon after this experience, while the Holy Spirit was speaking to her, that the same Spirit spoke to Andy and encouraged him to pick up on the clue of expressed weariness. Loretta, her daughter, and a number of her friends were baptized into the Seventh-day Adventist Church.

The tools used by the Holy Spirit, in this case, were Kenneth Cox videos. They were appropriate because Loretta was already watching Christian television programs, searching for light, and subsequently directed to the Bible by the Holy Spirit.

As depicted on the miner graphic (page 80), it is essential to use the right tools when one discovers a person who is being drawn by the Holy Spirit.

Attorney and Girlfriend See the Light

Pastor Morley asked for Pastor Tim to come to his city and help find those being drawn by the Holy Spirit. After prayer and claiming the promise of wisdom and guidance by the Holy Spirit, they went door-to-door. They had a brochure with pictures of well-known TV personages—Doug Batchelor and Mark Finley. They showed the brochure and said that they were telling folks about a new Christian TV station in the local area, as well as encouraging neighbors to participate in a spring Bible reading program.

They used a set of Bible lessons tied to local media. The brochure and heading on the Bible lessons both show graphics, TV channels, logos, etc. that tie the lessons with the media. This breaks down prejudice since television is a known public entity and non-threatening in the sense that they can turn it off if they desire. This leaves room for the Holy Spirit to do the drawing.

In about one hour's time, on three different days, they found ten people who accepted the Bible studies and agreed to weekly meetings at their doorstep to return filled-out lessons, go over questions, and receive more lessons. The Bible study guides were designed for the task. They were written to deal with contemporary issues such as threats of terrorism, war, economic stress, and political unrest.

At one house, a pleasant young man by the name of Garth accepted the lessons. On each appointed day, he met the pastors at the door with completed answer sheets. The pastors reviewed each lesson with Garth and gave him more study guides. After the third or fourth visit, Garth invited the pastors inside.

Pastor Tim reviewed the lessons on salvation and asked Garth if he understood. He said that he had attended a Christian law school, but never really heard about Jesus as a Savior. Pastor Tim gave his personal testimony and presented the gospel to Garth (see Supplement 1). He asked him if it made sense. Garth said that he could understand how God could pay the price for our sins, because he and other attorneys sometimes talk about how they "eat" the sins of those they defend, in the sense that they bear the guilt of the sins that criminals commit when they find ways to get them off the hook. He said that he felt guilty for setting some free who had actually committed crimes. He wondered if a person could be Christian and still be an attorney.

The pastors briefly gave their testimonies of accepting Christ. They assured Garth that they knew Christian attorneys and asked him if he would also like to accept Christ as his personal Savior. Garth responded, "Yes." Then they knelt and he repeated the prayer of reception after Pastor Tim.

They got up from their knees and Garth's girlfriend, Sheila, walked in the door with her three children. They chatted amiably for a bit, then Sheila said, "My mom says I am living like a pagan."

Pastor Tim recognized weariness in the tone of voice and concern about her mother's comment. He said, "Sheila, If Jesus were to come today, or if you were to die tonight, do you know for sure that you would be ready to go to heaven?"

Sheila exclaimed, "Last night I had a dream. I heard a great noise and got up and went to the window. The earth was shaking. I saw a bright light and knew Jesus was coming and I was not ready."

He further asked, "Do you have an idea what you would need to do in order to be ready?" Then he gave her a gospel presentation and asked if she would like to invite Jesus into her heart. Sheila responded in the affirmative.

After the gospel presentation and Sheila's prayer of reception, she was sobbing tears of joy. Garth was surprised. He thought he was the only one who needed to receive Jesus as a personal Savior since Sheila had been taking the kids to church.

In this case, media-oriented lessons were the tools used, as well as the gospel presentation.

The pastors continued to visit the couple in their home. They shared books with Garth. Friends from church held group Bible studies in Garth and Sheila's home.

They continued to study with the pastor. Garth was convicted from his study of the lessons that they should not be living together without being married. He moved out and went to live with his brother. Garth and his brother studied the Bible together, and he attended the SDA church near his brother's home. He proposed to Sheila. They were married, as well as baptized into the Seventh-day Adventist Church. Two of her children were baptized also.

If we review current available materials for evangelism and prayerfully consider each situation, the Lord will guide in the selection of the instrument to use to best feed expressed interest. He will also lead us to know the right time to offer Bible studies, books, DVDs, and Internet resources. The following list represents a few basic tools available for the gospel worker today:

Written Lessons

1. Gospel Presentation (available at jimkilmer.com)

2. *Come Alive* (available at Adventist Book Centers)—basic studies on salvation to follow the Gospel Presentation

3. *Stay Alive* (available at Adventist Book Centers)—follows the *Come Alive* lessons and covers basic doctrines

4. Media-oriented lessons, *e.g. He's Alive TV* (free to download at jimkilmer.com)

   • Contemporary issues

   • Righteousness by faith oriented

- First four lessons are a great follow up for the Gospel Presentation
- Designed to work with the mindset of evangelicals and lead them into the truth of the Sabbath and other distinctive doctrines from the standpoint of a relationship with Christ
- Introduce basic doctrines in a Christ-centered way

5. *Amazing Facts Bible Study Guides, Amazing Facts Advanced, Amazing Facts Bible Prophecy*
    - Colorful
    - Straightforward and hard-hitting on doctrine
    - Strong on conviction
    - The student either accepts the teachings or is in danger of rejecting the Holy Spirit
    - Joe Crews-and Doug Batchelor-type presentations that are clear, strong, and convincing
    - People who respond to these lessons often become solid, traditional Seventh-day Adventists.

6. *It is Written Evangelistic tools*—http://studies.itis-written.com/ (hard copies and online)
    - Discover Bible Studies
    - Every Word
    - My Place with Jesus
    - New Beginnings
    - The Search for Certainty
    - Unsealing Daniel's Mysteries

7. Voice of Prophecy Bible School—http://www.vop.com/article/854/site-categories/bible-school

8. Books and magazines; check local ABC for evangelistic books, tracts, and magazines

9. Health DVDs and videos, magazines, books

Chapter 20
How to Give Bible Studies

Some have a fearful view of soulwinning as though God were to say, "You have three minutes to create a mature stalk of ripe corn with tassels waving in the breeze. If you are not able to do it, I will be angry with you and cast you into hell fire."

This is shocking, blasphemous, ludicrous, and represents the voice of Satan trying to distort the picture of God and discourage the soulwinner.

The complete opposite is true. Power to convert souls does not lie in persuasive arguments, coercion, or contrived formulas. God does not ask us to pull a cigarette out of a person's mouth, walk into someone's house and throw the beer out of the refrigerator, or tie someone up and haul that person to church. The Holy Spirit can accomplish these radical changes in behavior, but we cannot.

The good news is that God does not expect you to create life in a person who is dead in trespasses and sins. You don't have to do the work of the Holy Spirit or perform the miracles witnessed in God's Word. All you need to do is plant the seed in the right place in season, tend the seed, remove weeds, water with the early and latter rain through prayer, and be ready to put in the sickle at the time of harvest.

> *Power to convert souls does not lie in persuasive arguments, coercion, or contrived formulas. God does not ask us to pull a cigarette out of a person's mouth, walk into someone's house and throw the beer out of the refrigerator, or tie someone up and haul that person to church. The Holy Spirit can accomplish these radical changes in behavior, but we cannot.*

The kingdom of God is as if a man should scatter seed on the ground, and should sleep by night and rise by day, and the seed should sprout and grow, he himself does not know how. For the earth yields crops by itself: first the blade, then the head, after that the full grain in the head. But when the grain ripens, immediately he puts in the sickle, because the harvest has come. (Mark 4:26–29)

These words of Jesus contain principles for giving effective Bible studies in the right sequence. First the seed of the gospel is planted in receptive soil. The seed grows as it feeds on the nutrients in the soil watered by the Holy Spirit. The farmer watches over the growing seed and feeds and waters it. He does not try to create the crop. The seed (word of God) produces fruit in the heart of the believer. The farmer enjoys the thought that he has done his work of planting and God will perform His miracle of producing growth. The diligent farmer's sleep is sweet. If he/she does not prepare the soil, plant the seed, water and weed, he/she might have a less restful night, especially as harvest time draws near.

This is good news for the gospel worker, for it narrows down his/her work to doable tasks. The farmer in the parable sows the seed, then sleeps. The seed grows in a mysterious, unexplainable way.

The gospel worker is to go forth with joy in happy contemplation of heavenly things. It does not require heroic effort to plant seed and then rest and let God work His miracles.

God gives the seed (His word). He awakens the awareness of need in the heart of the one for whom others have prayed. Our part is to discern, through the power of the Holy Spirit, the right time and place to plant the seed and the best seed to use. Then our work is to do the simple part that God entrusts to us.

When the burden of trying to play Creator rolls off our shoulders, God fills our hearts with joy and assurance. Rather than working in fear that God might kill us, we find that it "kills us" not to be active in witnessing.

Planting the Seed—Gospel Presentation

Even though God does not require the impossible from us, His plan does necessitate human and divine effort to prayerfully prepare and plant the seed.

Preparation includes cultivating the soil through prayer, friendship, deeds of kindness, and loving relationships. Often the most fertile soil lies within one's *oikos*. The gospel worker may be fortunate enough to find soil that has been cultivated by the media or seed planted by other Christians.

Preparation also includes becoming familiar with the types of seed and the right plant food (see Chapter 19). This means memorizing and practicing a gospel presentation (Supplement 1), accompanying one who is experienced, observing, and giving a gospel presentation. It includes the study of available materials and working through Bible study guides to know their content.

The hour of planting will require earnest endeavor. The enemy hates soulwinning. He will bring up scores of things to get in the way. Almost always the enemy will make it seem difficult to meet an appointment for Bible study. It is essential to push forward when you have a prayer commitment to give a gospel presentation and/or Bible study. I have seldom, if ever, given a gospel presentation without the enemy trying to interfere. Often there is a sense of reluctance, confusion, or a great distraction by some outside influence. A crying child, barking dog, or animated neighbor may suddenly appear. It is essential to be polite and acknowledge children, pets, neighbors, etc., then include them in the presentation, pray for strength, and resolutely push on. Rarely is it necessary to schedule another time, but if so, one can do it as a last resort when faced with overwhelming interruptions.

Tending the Seed

It is vital for the gospel worker to meet appointments for study promptly and faithfully. Let virtually nothing stand in your way. On rare occasions, it may be necessary to cancel an appointment. It is well to exchange phone numbers with your student in the event you need to cancel, and stay in touch for prayer and fellowship if appropriate.

Let the Bible do its work. Since the miracle-working power to convert souls is contained in the seed, it is essential to let it do its work (see Chapter 31). The secret is to let the Bible study guides spare your time and energy. It is better to review the lessons with the receptive students after they have filled in the blanks, rather than study with them text by text. The most effective Bible studies are those designed for the student to look up the Bible texts on their own and write their answers on the lines provided. This helps to foster habits of *personal* Bible study. You might go through a lesson or two with them to show them the procedure.

When you review the lessons with the student, if they have a wrong answer, don't discourage them by saying things like, "You got this one wrong." Instead say, "Let's look at the text again." Let them read the text. Often, they will discover the right answer. If they still have missed the point, you can say, "What do you think of this sentence in the text?"

You can be cordial and friendly, but don't let your Bible study time deteriorate into a mere gab fest. Precise times to begin and end encourage students to look forward to the next visit. They may be inclined to cancel the next study if they remember a long time spent the previous week.

Some students may ask questions that will be addressed in future lessons. It is best to postpone answers if possible. For example, one may ask, "What is the Mark of the Beast?" You can answer, "That is one of the most fascinating studies in the Bible. You will notice that it is number __ in the sequence. The lessons we are studying now will provide background and lead up to that topic." If the student's curiosity is satisfied without being grounded, the seed may fall on stony ground.

Watering. Pray for the early and latter rain for your own sake and that of the student (see Chapter 29). Teach the Bible student how to pray for wisdom, power, and guidance. A good set of Bible studies should have lessons on prayer and devotion.

Weeding. This requires a lot of attention and careful effort. Weeds may pop up from many directions and try to choke out the Bible study. Your student may have friends or family members that will object and try to discourage. The cares of this life may try to choke out study time. The following action plans help prevent and remove weeds:

- Agree to give top priority to study for a stated period of time, e.g. 14 weeks.

- Explain the parable of the sower and arrange a plan to deal with the cares of this life, stony ground, and other things that try to prevent study.

- Make a mutual commitment to give top priority to attendance.

- Warn about people who will try to distract.

- Warn about dissidents that will try to draw them away.

It is well to have the people with whom you are studying invite their family, friends, and neighbors to join the study. When these close family members and friends study the same material, it will be more difficult for them to try to convince the student that he/she is studying false doctrine.

Feeding. As you review the study guides on a weekly basis, you will find occasion to share your own experience of walking with Jesus, difficult decisions you have made, and rewards you have received. If the student is receptive, share good books about Christian experience. Introduce the Spirit of Prophecy, starting with *Steps to Christ, Thoughts from the Mount of Blessing, The Desire of Ages,* or *The Great Controversy.*

Harvest. The Holy Spirit ripens the crop for harvest, but the gospel worker must be ready to put in the sickle immediately when the crop is ready. Final harvest follows a series of decisions on the part of the recipient. First there is a decision to accept Christ as Savior. A discussion to study the Bible follows. Good Bible study guides have decision response questions for core beliefs.

The gospel worker takes note of attitudes and convictions, as well as marked responses on the study guides. Decisions follow a sequence. First comes understanding, then conviction, and finally action. The gospel worker does not try to do the work of the Holy Spirit, but can put in the sickle by asking questions to ascertain where the student is in his/her experience. You can ask, "Does this make sense?" "Is this clear?" Conviction will become evident in conversation and review of answers. The gospel worker may share his/her own experience of making decisions on the basis of conviction. One can ask, "Have you sensed God speaking to you through these texts?"

The action step is also between the student and the Holy Spirit. The gospel worker can ask, "Have you thought about keeping the Sabbath?" "Is there anything that would prevent you from being baptized?" "Where do you see yourself in reference to what we have studied about the remnant church?"

Most people who are converted face testing times concerning Sabbath observance and other key doctrines. It is best to explain that you cannot or will not tell them what to do. You can only share what Jesus said (see Chapter 31). Ask them to pray about it. Contact your prayer chain and expect a miracle.

Chapter 21
Mining Gold and Holding the Nugget

Another way of looking at soulwinning in the Spirit is through an illustration of a prospector who is always looking for gold. Once a vein of ore is located, the gospel worker mines that ore. Often when a person comes to the Lord, they have family and friends who are also interested. The soulwinner will concentrate time and energy in the area where gold has been found. Once the gold is discovered and mined, it is equally important to hold on to it.

Truth seekers may be led by the Holy Spirit, Bible study, and fellowship to attend Sabbath School and church. They may accept the entire message of the Bible and become baptized into the remnant church. However, it is at this point where the enemy often enters to disrupt, destroy, and snatch away the new members' faith. It is essential for gospel workers to cling to new believers and protect them as they would a most precious gold nugget.

Protecting Environment of Small Group SS Class

The Sabbath School Action Unit (see Supplement 3) provides a built-in weekly ground for the new believer to integrate with like disciples. Class members know how to provide a safe climate for growing Christians to ask questions and talk out their experiences. Class friendships and social activities help bind new members in love. The class focuses on life applications of God's Word, fellowship, prayer, nurture, and outreach. When class members share personal experience in the light of Scripture, new members, experienced Christians, and seekers all feed on Bread of Life together.

Gospel workers should teach new members what it means to be a disciple of Christ. A good Sabbath School class fosters ongoing support and training in personal ministry. Participation in ministries according to spiritual gifts helps graft new members into the body of Christ. Thus, a disciple-making cycle is set in operation. Jesus told His disciples to "go therefore and make disciples of all nations" (Matt. 28:18–20).

Disciple (definition)

A disciple is one who:

- is with Jesus and knows Him (Mark 3:14)

- abides in God's Word (John 8:31)
- believes in Jesus (John 2:11)
- learns to pray like Jesus (Luke 11:1)
- does what Jesus does (John 13:14–17; 2 Cor. 3:18)
- becomes like his teacher (Luke 6:40)
- becomes servant to all (Mark 10:42–45)
- denies self and follows Jesus (Matt. 16:24)
- gives up every earthly tie that would interfere with a relationship with Jesus (v. 25)
- takes up the cross of Christ daily (Luke 9:23–24)
- is filled with joy and the Holy Spirit (Acts 13:52)
- helps those in need (Acts 11:29)
- makes other disciples (Matt. 28:18–20)

Discipling New Members

Soon after baptism, the new believer is most often best prepared to accompany the gospel worker and learn how to study the Bible with others. The Apostle Paul told Timothy, "And the things that you have heard from me among many witnesses, commit these to faithful men who will be able to teach others also" (2 Tim. 2:2). If every soul that is won for Jesus would be taught how to disciple others, the church would grow exponentially. The new member brings in a whole new *oikos* which is often the most fertile field for evangelism. This is an arena well-suited to train the new disciple in soulwinning.

Protect Against Wolves in Sheep's Clothing

Correctors of Heretics: There are some church members who mean well, but are ignorant of how growth takes place in the lives of new converts. Some may be the first to go up to the new Christian and say things like, "That dress is too short." "You should not wear jewelry." These things need to be addressed prayerfully and with skill, not by external coercion.

Others may have little experience in reaching people of the world and may feel a need to show the new member the "satanic symbols" in the Sabbath School Study Guide and such. Yet others may zero in on the fine points of Jones, Waggoner, the 1888 Righteousness by Faith message, etc. The trustful and devout convert may be most vulnerable to the approach of those who have zeal without knowledge.

Unhealthy Reformers: Brand new converts are often interested in and have advanced information about healthful living, but some members may want to corner them and share the latest reasons for the grape cure, seaweed, raw foods, or other specialty or restricted diets.

Dissident Movements: The wolves that are most disguised in sheep's clothing are those who present themselves as loving, kind, gracious, and devout. They may want to draw the new convert off into special studies that promise to exalt Jesus. However, the hidden agenda is to accuse church leaders of apostasy and draw off members after themselves (see Acts 20:30).

The new member should be taught to be gracious but not taken in by extremes. The gospel worker will warn new members about wolves in sheep's clothing and tell the new members to politely let zealots know that they appreciate their good intentions, but will put those things on hold for a bit until they are well grounded in the basics.

Unscrupulous Business Deals

You would not think it possible, but there are some wolves in sheep's clothing that consider the trusting, new member a choice target for borrowing money and whatnot. Just like it is best not to do business with relatives, it is best not to do private business with church members unless there is an abundance of evidence that the business person is trustworthy. This does not mean that one should not patronize established businesses owned and operated by fellow church members.

(For additional guidelines on integrating new members, see Supplement 4.)

Prayerfully prospect for gold.

- Search for souls as for gold.
- Seek for interested people.
- Watch for indicators of spiritual weariness.
- Test the ground by observing how others respond to your Christian actions and expressions of faith.
- Ask your friends what they consider the secret of happiness, or what their philosophy of life is.
- Ask God for insight to be able to detect spiritual interest in those around you.
- Give your testimony when others ask you about your philosophy of life.

Follow the vein of ore.

- When you find interested people, spend your time with them.
- Interested people will often have family members and friends that will be interested.
- Don't move on until you have mined all the ore in the vein.

Do your major work with pockets of interested people.

- When you prepare a person for baptism, also teach them how to share the gospel with those within their spheres of interest.
- Use your most effective tools where there are pockets of interest.
- New members represent the growing edge of the church because they have their first love.
- One converted member brought thirty other family members with her through sharing videos.

Preserve nuggets of gold.

- Surround new members with love.
- Integrate new members into fellowship and ministry.
- Warn new members about those who would try to snatch them away.

Chapter 22
Quotes on Prayer

I am instructed to say to my fellow-workers, If you would have the rich treasures of heaven, you must hold secret communion with God. Unless you do this, your soul will be as destitute of the Holy Spirit as were the hills of Gilboa of dew and rain. When you hurry from one thing to another, when you have so much to do that you cannot take time to talk with God, how can you expect power in your work? (White, *Gospel Workers*, p. 272)

The path of sincerity and integrity is not a path free from obstruction, but in every difficulty we are to see a call to prayer. (White, *The Desire of Ages*, p. 667)

From the secret place of prayer came the power that shook the world in the Great Reformation. (White, *The Great Controversy*, p. 210)

The prayers of Christian mothers are not disregarded by the Father of all. (White, *My Life Today*, 21)

Those who decide to do nothing in any line that will displease God, will know after presenting their case before Him, just what course to pursue. (White, *The Desire of Ages*, p. 668)

There are long councils for devising plans, inventing new methods. There is a constant effort to get up entertainments to draw people to the church or the Sabbath school. Like the disciples, the workers raise the question, Shall we go to the villages and buy? What is the work to be done? Come unto Jesus. Humble faith and prayer will accomplish very much more than your long councils. (White, *Testimonies to Ministers and Gospel Workers*, p. 345)

If you have a large amount of work to do, then you have need of much prayer as well. If you have heavy burdens, then you are to seek the throne of God with greater earnestness; and as you seek after God, he takes your hand and lays it in his own. (White, *The Review and Herald*, January 5, 1911, par. 4)

Every day should come to us as the last day in which we may be privileged to work for God, and much of it must be given to prayer that we may work in the strength of Christ. This is the way in which Enoch walked with God, warning and condemning the world by manifesting before them a righteous character. (White, *The Review and Herald*, May 8, 1913, par. 6)

The meekness and love of Christ have been greatly lacking. A spirit of hurry has driven away the sweet spirit of Christ. More would have been done in the end, and in a much better manner, had more calmness been manifested…God is never in a hurry.

While the work should be pushed forward with persevering energy, it might better move more slowly than to be carried on in a spirit of hurry and friction, nervousness, and severe reprimands, which bring confusion and great unhappiness. (White, *Pamphlets*, No. 043, pp. 35–6)

And the promise of Christ's presence in answer to prayer should comfort and encourage his church today as much as it comforted and encouraged the apostles whom Christ directly addressed. (White, *The Spirit of Prophecy*, Vol. 3, p. 247)

Only the work accomplished with much prayer, and sanctified by the merit of Christ, will in the end prove to have been efficient for good. (White, *The Desire of Ages*, p. 362)

Chapter 23
The Baptism of the Holy Spirit

Have you longed to see greater miracles in evangelism in your family, neighborhood, and city? Have you prayed earnestly for loved ones, friends, neighbors, and Bible study interests? Have you wished that God would move in their lives in a more powerful way? If so, the baptism of the Holy Spirit promises to be a refreshing shower of heavenly blessing. Inspiring writings are full of rich promises in this regard (see Ron Clouzet, *Adventism's Greatest Need*, 2011). These promises, if rightly understood, do not lead to fanaticism, but to an increasingly joyous, purposeful life.

The baptism of the Holy Spirit is not an accomplishment to be showcased as an indication of our righteousness. It is given to those who realize their great need. It is not a trophy to be polished and placed on a shelf. The disciples who experienced Pentecost as promised by Jesus were common men with human weaknesses. Ten days of prayer for the baptism of the Holy Spirit made the difference between a Peter who could deny Christ with cursing and one who spoke with such power that thousands were converted. I believe the baptism of the Holy Spirit is an operational experience that takes place in the process of forming a union with Christ for ministry, not an end in itself. To focus primarily upon our own glorious experience may counter the work of the Holy Spirit.

Though the baptism of the Holy Spirit changes our desires and emotions, it is more about faith than feelings. Though love, joy, peace, and other aspects of the Spirit's fruit are byproducts, the main focus becomes the salvation of others rather than self-edification. The Holy Spirit searches the heart and refines like fire, yet results in abundant life rather than morbid introspection. The baptism of the Holy Spirit may involve significant time in prayer, but the length or intensity of prayer is a natural lifting of the heart to God in praise and intercession for others. It is not a contrived or forced work performed to get God's attention. Though humbling ourselves before God and surrender may be difficult, it paves the way for genuine repentance and an outflow of love and praise. It grows naturally as a result of rejoicing in the presence of our glorious Redeemer and appropriating His love and promises to our lives.

When we meditate upon the life of Christ and His wonderful promises in behalf of reaching our loved ones, prayer flows into joyous, Spirit-filled expressions of confidence, love, and compassion. We experience joy in the assimilation and actualization of the meditated Word of God in our lives. Whereas we may feel discomfort at first, this is what Isaiah, the Apostle Peter, and John the Revelator experienced in the presence of deity. After submission and surrender, however, the power comes from One who fulfills the role of Comforter with a baptism of love and assurance.

Some may wonder why it is necessary to spend time praying for the infilling of the Holy Spirit. Should we not simply accept by faith that the Holy Spirit is given in response to our prayers? It is true that humble faith and prayer operate with a childlike simplicity, yet increased power for witnessing is promised through something similar to what Jesus experienced on a daily basis and the disciples went through in the upper room. There is a supernatural power that accompanies sincere communion with God. Jesus spent considerable time in prayer and meditation. Why did He to do this? Notice the following quotes:

> As a man He [Jesus] supplicated the throne of God till His humanity was charged with a heavenly current that should connect humanity with divinity. Through continual communion He received life from God, that He might impart life to the world. His experience is to be ours. (White, *Desire of Ages*, p. 363)

> With strong crying and tears He [Jesus] sent His petitions to heaven, that His human nature might be strengthened, that He might be braced to meet the wily foe in all his deceptive workings, and fortified to fulfill His missions of uplifting humanity. To His workers He says, "I have given you an example, that ye should do as I have done." John 13:15. (White, *The Ministry of Healing*, p. 500)

I see this to be a joyous fellowship with God in devotional exercise, which is more like drinking from a fountain than trying to manufacture holiness.

The promise of power to win souls is precious indeed. Receiving the Holy Spirit in order to see the wayward individual turn to God is motivation enough for me to want to experience a deeper baptism.

> When God's people will believe, when they will turn their attention to that which is true, and living, and real, the Holy Spirit, in strong heavenly currents, will be poured upon the church. (White, *Manuscript Releases*, Vol. 2, p. 44)

> [After Pentecost,] Fields of labor were opened to be worked, and all found wherever they went in Christ's name, His representative in the Holy Spirit opened the hearts and doors for the disciples. (White, *Manuscript Releases*, Vol. 4, p. 337)

> The power of the Holy Spirit is drawing to God all who will be drawn. He is convincing men that the commandments of God are a life and death question with them. (White, *Manuscript Releases*, Vol. 4, p. 337)

The promise of power to win souls is precious indeed. Receiving the Holy Spirit in order to see the wayward individual turn to God is motivation enough for me to want to experience a deeper baptism.

Chapter 24
Cleansing Fire and New Creation

The enemy has inoculated society against receiving the converting power of the pure Word of God. The tide of social acceptance runs so strong and deep that millions are drifting out to sea as flotsam on its surface. Making a stand for distinctive truths is considered the most intolerable sin by the present generation. It is thought blasphemy to try to share biblical values with others. The same spirit of rebellion that removed a third of the angels from heaven has anchored the populous in the enticing deadly sin of self-gratification. This results in resistance to anything that does not pamper one's own selfish desires. We were told that it would be this way just before Jesus comes.

We sometimes forget, however, that similar challenges faced the disciples at the time of Christ. They were surrounded by the devil's strongholds. Were it not for the power of the Holy Spirit, the flood of evil would have been as overwhelming to them as it seems to us. Consider these words of inspiration:

> The Saviour knew that no argument, however logical, would melt hard hearts or break through the crust of worldliness and selfishness. He knew that His disciples must receive the heavenly endowment; that the gospel would be effective only as it was proclaimed by hearts made warm and lips made eloquent by a living knowledge of Him who is the way, the truth, and the life. The work committed to the disciples would require great efficiency; for the tide of evil ran deep and strong against them. A vigilant, determined leader was in command of the forces of darkness, and the followers of Christ could battle for the right only through the help that God, by His Spirit, would give them. (White, *The Acts of the Apostles*, p. 31)

We sometimes forget, however, that similar challenges faced the disciples at the time of Christ. They were surrounded by the devil's strongholds. Were it not for the power of the Holy Spirit, the flood of evil would have been as overwhelming to them as it seems to us.

When we pray for the baptism of the Holy Spirit as did the early disciples, we can expect the promises of God's Word to be fulfilled. The Godhead in fullness will become real to us. However, as was true of the coming of the Messiah, the Comforter begins His work by confronting sin. Concerning the promise of the Messiah, the prophet declared, "But who can endure the day of His coming? And who can stand when He appears? For He *is* like a refiner's fire and like launderers' soap" (Mal. 3:2). The same is true of the third member of the Godhead.

John the Baptist said, "I indeed baptize you with water; but One mightier than I is coming, whose sandal strap I am not worthy to loose. He will baptize you with the Holy Spirit and fire" (Luke 3:16). Fire refines away the dross and cleanses impurities. We must first allow the Holy Spirit to do His work of cleansing our own hearts before we can reach out to others. Speaking of the Holy Spirit, Jesus promised His disciples, "And when He has come, He will convict the world of sin, and of righteousness, and of judgment" (John 16:8). Power for witnessing begins with the prayer. "Search me, O God, and know my heart; Try me, and know my anxieties; And see if *there is any* wicked way in me…" (Ps. 139:23, 24).

Pastor Dwight Nelson said that when he prayed this prayer, it was like a video of his shortcomings was displayed before him. Before, he could not think of any commandment that he was violating. He was serving as a faithful minister of the gospel with his sermons reaching millions, yet the Sprit revealed imperfect qualities that were hidden from his view. He said that when he saw these faults, confessed, and laid them upon the spotless Lamb of God, he rose from his knees feeling more peace than he ever experienced.

The baptism of the Holy Spirit is a baptism of assurance and love. It is a baptism of the righteousness of Christ applied in full measure, but the path of peace is sometimes a path of painful surrender. Before we can cry out for the assurance of salvation with strong conviction, we must first be confronted with our utter helplessness. Our true condition is often hidden from our eyes.

Meditation on the life of Jesus as revealed in inspired writings, as well as on the Ten Commandments, will help reveal our need. The words of the prophets, ancient and recent, pierce our hearts and open blind eyes. Straight testimonies cut through the fog of shallow theology. The Holy Spirit will expose our friendship with the world and yearning for the things of man rather than the things of God. Our strife for supremacy, as well as our indifference, defensiveness, and peevishness will appear in contrast to the pure, perfect love of Christ.

This is an individual matter. The sins of one are not the sins of another. When we pray and meditate on Scripture, we must be ready to receive the conviction of the Holy Spirit. This conviction must come from a clear "Thus says the Lord" however, not from a false, over-sensitive conscience. Sometimes it takes much prayer, heart searching, and study to detect the difference between the conviction of the Holy Spirit and the accusations of the enemy. The devil will try to pervert or counterfeit the work of the Holy Spirit and get us to either ignore shortcomings or dwell upon them in a melancholic way. If we resist the conviction of the Holy Spirit, we may feel a false sense of security, flattering ourselves that everything is okay, when we are simply blind to our needs. We arc told, "The more closely you live to God, the more clearly will you discern your weaknesses and your dangers" (White, *Testimonies for the Church*, Vol. 3, p. 321).

> The closer you come to Jesus, the more faulty you will appear in your own eyes; for your vision will be clearer, and your imperfections will be seen in broad and distinct contrast to His perfect nature. This is evidence that Satan's delusions have lost their power; that the vivifying influence of the Spirit of God is arousing you. (White, *Steps to Christ*, pp. 64–5)

The solution, however, is always the same. We must look away from ourselves to Christ for cleansing and a change of heart. If we try to carry the burden of revealed sins, it will overwhelm us. Jesus promised that He would intercede on our behalf for the Holy Spirit. Not only did Jesus promise that the Holy Spirit would bring conviction of sins, but also comfort for sins forgiven. We will understand more of His intercessory work than ever. We will see that our claim for righteousness and worthiness to receive the Holy Spirit is based on His accomplished work on the cross. We will humble our hearts in true repentance, restore broken relationships, and confess our faults one to another. We will recognize and confess our unbelief. We will receive the spirit of adoption and allow the Holy Spirit to put to death the deeds of the flesh (see Rom. 8:12–15).

We will also be convicted of our right standing with God in the judgment with the assurance that the prince of this world has been judged (see John 16:11). We will receive the same confirmation for ministry that Jesus received when He was baptized by the Holy Spirit. That is the assurance that we are sons and daughters of God in the fullest sense, and that God looks upon the righteousness of Christ in our behalf. We will be convinced that since we were in Christ at His baptism, and on the cross, God says of each of us, "This is my beloved son [or daughter], in whom I am well pleased." The Holy Spirit will testify with our spirit that we are indeed the children of God (see Rom. 8:16). The following quotes speak of these realities:

I am feeling very free and peaceful. I feel the precious love of Christ in my heart. It humbles me in my own sight, while Jesus is exalted before me. Oh, how I do long for that social and mysterious connection with Jesus that elevates us above the temporal things of life. It is my anxiety to be right with God, to have His Spirit continually witnessing with me that I am indeed a child of God. (White, *Selected Messages*, Book 3, p. 105)

God desires to refresh His people by the gift of the Holy Spirit, baptizing them anew in His love. There is no need for a dearth of the Spirit in the church. After Christ's ascension the Holy Spirit came upon the waiting, praying, believing disciples with a fullness and power that reached every heart. In the future the earth is to be lightened with the glory of God. A holy influence is to go forth to the world from those who are sanctified through the truth. The earth is to be encircled with an atmosphere of grace. The Holy Spirit is to work on human hearts, taking the things of God and showing them to men. (White, *Testimonies for the Church*, Vol. 9, p. 40)

God will bless all who thus prepare themselves for His service. They will understand what it means to have the assurance of the Spirit because they have received Christ by faith. (White, *Testimonies for the Church*, Vol. 6, p. 363)

Chapter 25
Eyewitness Account of the Upper Room Experience

We have a record of what took place in the hearts and lives of those assembled in the upper room who received the baptism of the Holy Spirit. This comes from one who was taken there in vision. These quotes are taken from *The Acts of the Apostles* by E.G. White:

> In obedience to Christ's command, they waited in Jerusalem for the promise of the Father--the outpouring of the Spirit. They did not wait in idleness. The record says that they were "continually in the temple, praising and blessing God." Luke 24:53. They also met together to present their requests to the Father in the name of Jesus. They knew that they had a Representative in heaven, an Advocate at the throne of God. In solemn awe they bowed in prayer, repeating the assurance, "Whatsoever ye shall ask the Father in My name, He will give it you. Hitherto have ye asked nothing in My name: ask, and ye shall receive, that your joy may be full." John 16:23, 24. Higher and still higher they extended the hand of faith, with the mighty argument, "It is Christ that died, yea rather, that is risen again, who is even at the right hand of God, who also maketh intercession for us." Romans 8:34.
>
> As the disciples waited for the fulfillment of the promise, they humbled their hearts in true repentance and confessed their unbelief. As they called to remembrance the words that Christ had spoken to them before His death they understood more fully their meaning. Truths which had passed from their memory were again brought to their minds, and these they repeated to one another. They reproached themselves for their misapprehension of the Saviour. Like a procession, scene after scene of His wonderful life passed before them. As they meditated upon His pure, holy life they felt that no toil would be too hard, no sacrifice too great, if only they could bear witness in their lives to the loveliness of Christ's character. Oh, if they could but have the past three years to live over, they thought, how differently they

would act! If they could only see the Master again, how earnestly they would strive to show Him how deeply they loved Him, and how sincerely they sorrowed for having ever grieved Him by a word or an act of unbelief! But they were comforted by the thought that they were forgiven. And they determined that, so far as possible, they would atone for their unbelief by bravely confessing Him before the world.

The disciples prayed with intense earnestness for a fitness to meet men and in their daily intercourse to speak words that would lead sinners to Christ. Putting away all differences, all desire for the supremacy, they came close together in Christian fellowship. They drew nearer and nearer to God, and as they did this they realized what a privilege had been theirs in being permitted to associate so closely with Christ. Sadness filled their hearts as they thought of how many times they had grieved Him by their slowness of comprehension, their failure to understand the lessons that, for their good, He was trying to teach them.

These days of preparation were days of deep heart searching. The disciples felt their spiritual need and cried to the Lord for the holy unction that was to fit them for the work of soul saving. They did not ask for a blessing for themselves merely. They were weighted with the burden of the salvation of souls. They realized that the gospel was to be carried to the world, and they claimed the power that Christ had promised.

During the patriarchal age the influence of the Holy Spirit had often been revealed in a marked manner, but never in its fullness. Now, in obedience to the word of the Saviour, the disciples offered their supplications for this gift, and in heaven Christ added His intercession. He claimed the gift of the Spirit, that He might pour it upon His people. (pp. 35–37)

Those who at Pentecost were endued with power from on high, were not thereby freed from further temptation and trial. As they witnessed for truth and righteousness they were repeatedly assailed by the enemy of all truth, who sought to rob them of their Christian experience. They were compelled to strive with all their God-given powers to reach the measure of the stature of men and women in Christ Jesus. Daily they prayed for fresh supplies of grace, that they might reach higher and still higher toward perfection. Under the Holy Spirit's working even the weakest, by exercising faith in God, learned to improve their entrusted powers and to become sanctified, refined, and ennobled. As in humility they submitted to the molding influence of the Holy Spirit, they received of the fullness of the Godhead and were fashioned in the likeness of the divine. (pp. 49–50)

Since this is the means by which we are to receive power, why do we not hunger and thirst for the gift of the Spirit? Why do we not talk of it, pray for it, and preach concerning it? The Lord is more willing to give the Holy Spirit to those who serve Him than parents are to give good gifts to their children. For the daily baptism of the Spirit every worker should offer his petition to God. Companies of Christian workers should gather to ask for special help, for heavenly wisdom, that they may know how to plan and execute wisely. Especially should they pray that God will baptize His chosen ambassadors in mission fields with a rich measure of His Spirit. The presence of the Spirit with God's workers will give the proclamation of truth a power that not all the honor or glory of the world could give.

With the consecrated worker for God, in whatever place he may be, the Holy Spirit abides. The words spoken to the disciples are spoken also to us. The Comforter is ours as well as theirs. The Spirit furnishes the strength that sustains striving, wrestling souls in every emergency, amidst the hatred of the world, and the realization of their own failures and mistakes. In sorrow and affliction, when the outlook seems dark and the future perplexing, and we feel helpless and alone,—these are the times when, in answer to the prayer of faith, the Holy Spirit brings comfort to the heart.

It is not a conclusive evidence that a man is a Christian because he manifests spiritual ecstasy under extraordinary circumstances. Holiness is not rapture: it is an entire surrender of the will to God; it is living by every word that proceeds from the mouth of God; it is doing the will of our heavenly Father; it is trusting God in trial, in darkness as well as in the light; it is walking by faith and not by sight; it is relying on God with unquestioning confidence, and resting in His love. (pp. 50–1)

The office of the Holy Spirit is distinctly specified in the words of Christ: "When He is come, He will reprove the world of sin, and of righteousness, and of judgment." John 16:8. It is the Holy Spirit that convicts of sin. If the sinner responds to the quickening influence of the Spirit, he will be brought to repentance and aroused to the importance of obeying the divine requirements. (p. 52)

Having brought conviction of sin, and presented before the mind the standard of righteousness, the Holy Spirit withdraws the affections from the things of this earth and fills the soul with a desire for holiness. "He will guide you into all truth" (John 16:13), the Saviour declared. If men are willing to be molded, there will be brought about a sanctification of the whole being. The Spirit will take the things of God and stamp them on the soul. By His power the way of life will be made so plain that none need err therein. (pp. 52–3)

And today God is still using His church to make known His purpose in the earth. Today the heralds of the cross are going from city to city, and from land to land, preparing the way for the second advent of Christ. The standard of God's law is being exalted. The Spirit of the Almighty is moving upon men's hearts, and those who respond to its influence become witnesses for God and His truth. In many places consecrated men and women may be seen communicating to others the light that has made plain to them the way of salvation through Christ. And as they continue to let their light shine, as did those who were baptized with the Spirit on the Day of Pentecost, they receive more and still more of the Spirit's power. Thus the earth is to be lightened with the glory of God. (pp. 53–4)

Those only who are constantly receiving fresh supplies of grace, will have power proportionate to their daily need and their ability to use that power. Instead of looking forward to some future time when, through a special endowment of spiritual power, they will receive a miraculous fitting up for soul winning, they are yielding themselves daily to God, that He may make them vessels meet for His use. Daily they are improving the opportunities for service that lie within their reach. Daily they are witnessing for the Master wherever they may be, whether in some humble sphere of labor in the home, or in a public field of usefulness. (p. 55)

To the repentant sinner, hungering and thirsting for righteousness, the Holy Spirit reveals the Lamb of God that taketh away the sin of the world. "He shall receive of Mine, and shall show it unto you," Christ said. "He shall teach you all things, and bring all things to your remembrance, whatsoever I have said unto you." John 16:14; 14:26.

The Spirit is given as a regenerating agency, to make effectual the salvation wrought by the death of our Redeemer. The Spirit is constantly seeking to draw the attention of men to the great offering that was made on the cross of Calvary, to unfold to the world the love of God, and to open to the convicted soul the precious things of the Scriptures. (p. 52)

Chapter 26
Baptism of the Holy Spirit and the Latter Rain

There are linking texts that tie the baptism of the Holy Spirit on the day of Pentecost with the promise of the outpouring of the Holy Spirit in Joel (compare Acts 2:16–21 and Joel 2:28–32). The text in Joel refers to the "last days," so it must have a dual application, pointing forward to our day as well.

Throughout the Bible, the work of the Holy Spirit is illustrated by many types and symbols. The "early and latter rain" are symbols of the Holy Spirit that are related to seed time and harvest (see Deut. 11:14; Jer. 5:23–25; James 5:7). We are admonished to ask the Lord for rain in the time of the latter rain (see Zech. 10:1).

The latter rain and righteousness by faith are related. Isaiah says, "Rain down, you heavens, from above, And let the skies pour down righteousness; Let the earth open, let them bring forth salvation, and let righteousness spring up together. I, the Lord, have created it" (45:8). Hosea declares, "Sow for yourselves righteousness; Reap in mercy; Break up your fallow ground, For *it is* time to seek the LORD, Till He comes and rains righteousness on you" (10:12). He also writes, "Then shall we know, if we follow on to know the LORD: his going forth is prepared as the morning; and he shall come unto us as the rain, as the latter and former rain unto the earth" (6:3, KJV).

We can expect that Holy Spirit baptism will bring home as never before the righteousness of Christ that comes through His blood alone. The Prophet Joel declared, "So rejoice, O sons of Zion, And be glad in the Lord your God; For He has given you the early rain for your vindication. And He has poured down for you the rain, the early and latter rain as before" (2:23, NASB). Inspired statements like the following link righteousness by faith and the latter rain.

Many had lost sight of Jesus. They needed to have their eyes directed to His divine person, His merits, and His changeless love for the human family. All power is given into His

The latter rain and righteousness by faith are related.

hands, that He may dispense rich gifts unto men, imparting the priceless gift of His own righteousness to the helpless human agent. This is the message that God commanded to be given to the world. It is the third angel's message, which is to be proclaimed with a loud voice, and attended with the outpouring of His Spirit in a large measure. (White, *Testimonies to Ministers and Gospel Workers*, p. 92)

The time of test is just upon us, for the loud cry of the third angel has already begun in the revelation of the righteousness of Christ, the sin-pardoning Redeemer. This is the beginning of the light of the angel whose glory shall fill the whole earth. (White, *Selected Messages*, Book 1, p. 363)

Are our supplications ascending to God in living faith? Are we opening the door of the heart to Jesus and closing every means of entrance to Satan? Are we daily obtaining clearer light and greater strength, that we may stand in Christ's righteousness? Are we emptying our hearts of all selfishness, and cleansing them, preparatory to receiving the latter rain from heaven? (White, *In Heavenly Places*, p. 348)

The revelation of Christ by the Holy Spirit brought to them a realizing sense of his power and majesty, and they stretched forth their hands unto him by faith, saying, "I believe." Thus it was in the time of the early rain; but the latter rain will be more abundant. The Saviour of men will be glorified, and the earth will be lightened with the bright shining of the beams of his righteousness. He is the fountain of light, and light from the gates ajar has been shining upon the people of God, that they may lift him up in his glorious character before those who sit in darkness....They have not opened the heart to receive the grace of Christ; they know not the operation of the Spirit; they are as meal without leaven; for there is no working principle in all their labor, and they fail to win souls to Christ. They do not appropriate the righteousness of Christ; it is a robe unworn by them, a fullness unknown, a fountain untouched. (White, *The Review and Herald*, November 29, 1892, par. 6)

The great outpouring of the Spirit of God, which lightens the whole earth with His glory, will not come until we have an enlightened people, that know by experience what it means to be laborers together with God. When we have entire, wholehearted consecration to the service of Christ, God will recognize the fact by an outpouring of His Spirit without measure; but this will not be while the largest portion of the church are not laborers together with God. God cannot pour out His Spirit when selfishness and self-indulgence are so manifest; when a spirit prevails that, if put into words, would express that answer of Cain, "Am I my brother's keeper?" (White, *Counsels on Stewardship*, p. 52)

I believe that many may have experienced and are experiencing the baptism of the Holy Spirit, perhaps without recognizing it as such. However, inspired counsel encourages greater and still greater entreaties for manifestations of power.

There needs to be a waking up among God's people, that His work may be carried forward with power. We need the baptism of the Holy Spirit. We need to understand that God will add to the ranks of His people men of ability and influence, who are to act their part in warning the world. All in the world are not lawless and sinful. God has many thousands who have not bowed the knee to Baal. There are God-fearing men in the fallen churches. If this were not so, we should not be given the message to bear, "Babylon the great is fallen, is fallen....Come out of her, My people." (White, *Evangelism*, 558–9)

Some may question why we should continue praying for the outpouring of the Holy Spirit, since God hears our simple prayers and will give the latter rain when the time is right. Why does the Bible say, "And give Him no rest till He establishes and till He makes Jerusalem a praise in the earth" (Isa. 62:7). It is not God who needs to be reminded, but we who need a deeper experience in asking. Consider these statements:

> The third angel's message is swelling into a loud cry, and you must not feel at liberty to neglect the present duty, and still entertain the idea that at some future time you will be the recipients of great blessing, when without any effort on your part a wonderful revival will take place.... Today you are to have your vessel purified, that it may be ready for the heavenly dew, ready for the showers of the latter rain; for the latter rain will come, and the blessing of God will fill every soul that is purified from every defilement. It is our work today to yield our souls to Christ, that we may be fitted for the time of refreshing from the presence of the Lord—fitted for the baptism of the Holy Spirit. (White, *Evangelism*, pp. 701–2)

> Will we carry forward the work in the Lord's way? Are we willing to be taught of God? Will we wrestle with God in prayer? Will we receive the baptism of the Holy Spirit? This is what we need and may have at this time. Then we shall go forth with a message from the Lord, and the light of truth will shine forth as a lamp that burneth, reaching to all parts of the world. If we will walk humbly with God, God will walk with us. Let us humble our souls before Him, and we shall see of His salvation. (White, *Fundamentals of Christian Education*, p. 532)

> We need to cry to God as did Jacob for a fuller baptism of the Holy Spirit. The time for labor is short. Let there be much praying. Let the soul yearn after God. Let the secret places of prayer be often visited. Let there be a taking hold of the strength of the Mighty One of Israel (White, *Historical Sketches of the Foreign Missions of the Seventh-day Adventists*, p. 294).

> O that the baptism of the Holy Spirit might come upon you, that you might be imbued with the Spirit of God! Then day by day you will become more and more conformed to the image of Christ, and in every action of your life the question would be, "Will it glorify my Master?" (White, *My Life Today*, 49)

> Many present the doctrines and theories of our faith; but their presentation is as salt without savor; for the Holy Spirit is not working through their faithless ministry. They have not opened the heart to receive the grace of Christ; they know not the operation of the Spirit; they are as meal without leaven; for there is no working principle in all their labor, and they fail to win souls to Christ. They do not appropriate the righteousness of Christ; it is a robe unworn by them, a fullness unknown, a fountain untouched. (White, *Evangelism*, p. 697)

Chapter 27
The Promise of the Spirit Fulfilled

Why could Pastor Dalton (chapters 14 and 28) answer Mrs. Schmidt so confidently, declaring that he had been baptized by the Holy Spirit without speaking in tongues? He did not know how to answer from the Bible until he opened his mouth to speak. As he spoke, an overall understanding of the nature of Holy Spirit baptism came into his mind as he gave testimony to receiving that baptism. Many of the following biblical passages came together at the moment of need according to the promise. I am not saying that the Lord will bring to mind what we have not studied, but I believe the pastor was being prompted by the Holy Spirit as promised in the following quote:

> As the messengers of the Lord present these solemn truths, they must realize that they are handling subjects of eternal interest, and they should seek for the baptism of the Holy Spirit, that they may speak, not their own words, but the words given them by God. (White, *To Be Like Jesus*, p. 69)

After his experience with Mrs. Schmidt, you can imagine how urgent and important it became for Pastor Dalton to diligently go on searching the Scriptures concerning the baptism of the Holy Spirit. He found only a few texts in the Bible that specifically mention it. John the Baptist indicated that Jesus would baptize with the Holy Spirit and fire (see Matt. 3:11; Mark 1:8; Luke 3:16; John 1:33). When Jesus appeared to the disciples prior to ascending to Heaven, He reminded them that He had promised to send the Comforter, and now they should wait for the promise (see Acts 1:4, 5). The only scriptural reference to the promise of the baptism of the Holy Spirit by Jesus is contained in the above texts, but John 14, 15, and 16 contain details of what the Holy Spirit would do when He would come to the disciples. Some may ask how we know that the promises of these chapters concerning the Holy Spirit were detailing Pentecost.

There are a number of evidences that link the promise of the Spirit by Jesus and what happened on the day of Pentecost: 1) John 14:16—Jesus said that He would pray to the Father, who would send another Comforter. John says that the Holy Spirit was given *after* Jesus ascended to heaven and was glorified (see 7:39). Paul indicates that when Jesus ascended to heaven, He gave gifts to men (see Eph. 4:8, 11). He then goes on to list several gifts of the Holy Spirit. Therefore, the promise of Jesus to send the Holy Spirit must have been fulfilled on the day of Pentecost. 2) John 15:26, 27—Jesus promised that when the Holy Spirit would come from the Father, He would testify of Jesus and the disciples would bear witness. In the upper room, Jesus promised power for witnessing when they would receive the baptism of the Holy Spirit (see Acts 1:8). He told them to wait for the promise of the Father which they had heard from Him. This must have been the promise in John 14. He then went on to promise the baptism of the Holy Spirit (see Acts 1:5). Therefore, John 14, 15, and 16 must constitute a description of what the Holy Spirit would do when He baptized them. When Jesus makes a promise, He keeps it. Therefore, we should find in John's chapters explanations of what it means to experience the baptism of the Holy Spirit.

Chapter 28
Baptism of the Holy Spirit and Speaking in Tongues

The question of speaking in tongues in relationship to the baptism of the Holy Spirit cannot be answered by anything but the Bible. In conversation with Mrs. Schmidt, for example, Pastor Dalton knew it would not help to share the testimony of a man he met who had been a practicing spiritualist medium. The former spiritualist said that before becoming a Christian, he spoke in tongues in séances, and it was the same as what he experienced in Pentecostal churches and hippie communes.

Pastor Dalton knew the answer must come from clear, biblical teaching. He had reviewed Paul's letter to the Corinthian church. The Apostle Paul says, "I thank my God I speak with tongues more than you all" (1 Cor. 14:18).

The text of 1 Corinthians 14 makes a clear case against speaking in an unknown tongue in church, but texts like the following may at first sound as though Paul may have spoken in an unknown tongue in private at home, "For he who speaks in a tongue does not speak to men but to God, for no one understands *him;* however, in the spirit he speaks mysteries" (14:2). If one takes the text literally, it says that *no one* understands him, he speaks *mysteries,* and the petitioner is not speaking to men but to God, so how could it be a known tongue? It further complicates the picture that on two occasions after Pentecost, it says that when people received the Holy Spirit, they spoke with tongues without reference to people hearing in their own language (see Acts 10:44–46; 19:6). However, I do not believe that Paul spoke in an unknown tongue in church or in private.

I believe that when Paul said he spoke in tongues more than the others, he was speaking of known languages like Greek, Hebrew, Aramaic, and Latin. Some may ask how Paul could be referring to speaking known languages when he says, "For if I pray in a tongue, my spirit prays, but my understanding is unfruitful" (1 Cor. 14:14).

I believe it is consistent with Scripture that when Paul is writing about prayer, he is using a rhetorical "I" when he says "if I pray in a tongue." He is not saying that he does, but *if* he were to speak in an unknown tongue, his spirit may pray, but his understanding would be unfruitful. He then goes on to say that the person who prays to God in an *unknown* tongue speaks mysteries that no one understands. He does not actually say that he does this. He does not say it is good for people to do it. Rather, his point is that prayer with understanding is better. I also believe that the new believers in Acts 10 and 19 likely spoke in known tongues. However, it is difficult to, on the basis of Scripture, convince people of this, especially when they have experienced a supernatural, ecstatic utterance and are convinced that it is from God. This is where the power of the Holy Spirit is essential.

These were some of the difficult passages that were in mind when Pastor Dalton studied with Mrs. Schmidt. Only the Holy Spirit could use the Scripture in such a powerful manner to declare that unknown tongues are not to be used in communicating the gospel, but doctrine is essential. The following quote underscores the fact that Pentecost is essential for witnessing:

> A vigilant, determined leader was in command of the forces of darkness, and the followers of Christ could battle for the right only through the help that God, by His Spirit, would give them. (White, *The Acts of the Apostles*, p. 31)

The enemy has made soulwinning increasingly difficult. He can blind eyes and use Scripture in such a manner to support confusion. We not only deal with the confused concepts and misunderstandings of souls held captive by the enemy, but we face the invisible master deceiver. For this reason, we need a genuine baptism of the Holy Spirit as the servant of the Lord says:

> As we near the end of time, falsehood will be so mingled with truth, that only those who have the guidance of the Holy Spirit will be able to distinguish truth from error. We need to make every effort to keep the way of the Lord. We must in no case turn from His guidance to put our trust in man. The Lord's angels are appointed to keep strict watch over those who put their faith in the Lord, and these angels are to be our special help in every time of need. Every day we are to come to the Lord with full assurance of faith, and to look to Him for wisdom....Those who are guided by the Word of the Lord will discern with certainty between falsehood and truth, between sin and righteousness. (White, *God's Amazing Grace*, p. 201)

I entreat the church members in every city that they lay hold upon the Lord with determined effort for the baptism of the Holy Spirit. Be assured that Satan is not asleep. Every obstacle possible he will place in the way of those who would advance in this work. Too often these obstacles are regarded as insurmountable. Let everyone now be soundly and truly converted, and then lay hold of the work intelligently and with faith. (White, *Counsels on Health*, p. 548)

We must have the holy unction from God; we must have the baptism of the Holy Spirit; for this is the only efficient agent in the promulgation of sacred truth. Yet this is what we most lack. The divine power combined with human effort, connection first and last and ever with God, the source of our strength, is absolutely necessary in our work. We must hang our whole weight on the world's Redeemer; he must be our dependence for strength. Without this, all our efforts will be unavailing. Even now the time has come when we must recognize this fully, or we shall be outgeneraled by a powerful, cunning foe. We must connect more closely with God; and all our plans and arrangements must be in harmony with his plans, or they will not prove effectual. (White, *The Review and Herald*, Dec. 15, 1885, par. 2)

> **The enemy has made soulwinning increasingly difficult. He can blind eyes and use Scripture in such a manner to support confusion.**

Chapter 29
Prayer That Reaches Souls for Christ

Why pray for the lost? We know it makes a difference when we pray, but why? Since people will do what they choose, what difference does it make when we pray for them? How, we might ask, can the prayer of one human being impact something as seemingly intangible and private as the faith of another? Part of the answer comes from understanding the dynamics of the great controversy. We are told that Jesus prayed for Peter. "Simon, Simon, behold, Satan hath desired to have you, that he may sift you as wheat. But I have prayed for you, that your faith fail not" (Luke 22:31, 32, KJV). The prayer of Christ made a counter-claim to Satan's claim on Peter.

Satan accuses mankind day and night (see Rev. 12:10). He uses God's perfect righteousness and fairness as arguments against the salvation of the lost. This fact is implied in several New Testament verses. Paul says:

> [W]hom God set forth *as* a propitiation by His blood, through faith, to demonstrate His righteousness, because in His forbearance God had passed over the sins that were previously committed, to demonstrate at the present time His righteousness, that He might be just and the justifier of the one who has faith in Jesus. (Romans 3:25, 26)

In other words, it is, in all fairness, essential that God acts in a righteous way. Satan accused God of being selfish in saving sinners.

Satan claims that God should not answer our prayers because He is perfect and just and it is not fair for us to ask since we have sinned. When Jesus accepts the blame or consequence of our sin, it removes this argument. Our sin was hurled at the innocent Lamb of God. His blood flowed forth in consequence. This removes Satan's argument against the justice of God. God was justified in saving us and answering our prayers because He assumed the blame for our sins. Satan casts his accusation against us, but it falls upon Jesus. Our sin takes the life of Christ. God takes the blame for our sins. The accuser of the brethren is cast down. Our part is to believe in His act of justification.

Satan also claims ownership of the entire human race because every human, except Christ, has sinned (see Rom. 3:23). A person becomes subject to one to whom he/she yields (see Rom. 6:16). Christ's perfect life of obedience in our human flesh refutes Satan's claim that the entire race has chosen Satan's ways (see John 14:30).

Faith is essential for answered prayer (see Heb. 11:6). It demonstrates an attitude toward God that shows harmony with divine principles of love. This is also an argument against Satan's claims.

Faith is not feeling, but a connection with God that involves not only trust, confidence, and expectancy, but also love and obedience (see James 2:14–26; Gal. 5:6). This is why faith is not something that we can produce. It is supernaturally endowed as a gift (see Eph. 2:8). Everyone has been given a measure of faith (see Rom. 12:3). Faith is imparted through the divine power of God's word (see 10:17), as well as the supernatural operation of the Holy Spirit (see Gal. 5:22). The reformers saw prayer as the chief exercise of faith. When we pray for others, faith is exercised.

The enemy knows that faith is the key ingredient for answered prayer, so he tries to get us to manufacture a feeling or assume God will answer even if we are not surrendered to His will. Satan works to bring about fear, which is related to doubt (see Rev. 21:8). This is one of Satan's greatest weapons. It is the work of the devil to draw the soul away from belief through deception (see 1 Tim. 4:1). The intercessory work of Christ in the heavenly sanctuary refutes this snare. I have been in war situations where I was so overwhelmed with circumstances that words of prayer would hardly come out of my mouth (see my book, *Angels in No-man's Land*). The enemy was on hand to try to tell me that this was evidence that God could not hear my prayer. However, I found comfort in the fact that I have an Intercessor who is not limited by my feelings or fears. Without an understanding of the high-priestly ministry of Christ, we will not have faith to go through the final crisis.

The subject of the sanctuary and the investigative judgment should be clearly understood by the people of God. All need a knowledge for themselves of the position and work of their great High Priest. Otherwise, it will be impossible for them to exercise the faith which is essential at this time, or to occupy the position which God designs them to fill. (White, *Evangelism*, pp. 221–2)

How does this apply to prayers for the lost? God will not force the will of those walking away from Christ, but prayer for them allows God to open the eyes of their understanding (see Eph. 1:16–18) and do a work on the hearts of the lost (see 3:16–19). He has a right to do this because He has answered the accusations of the enemy, and because the petitioner exercises faith which is harmonious with God's character.

We cannot manufacture faith, but we can ask for it by praying for the Holy Spirit (see Luke 11:13), confessing that we lack it (see Mark 9:24), and reading and meditating on God's Word (see Rom. 10:17). We can exercise the faith that we do have by claiming God's promises.

In the perfect government of God, it is right and just for Him to respond to requests from those who are in harmony with righteousness (see James 5:16). The very act of intercession demonstrates love. This act is an argument against Satan's claims that God is unfair. Both the salvific act of Jesus and our love poured forth in prayer demonstrate unselfishness. This demonstration gives God just cause to open blind eyes and deliver hearts held captive by Satan (see Isa. 49:24, 25). This will not force the choice of the lost, but restore their power to choose God. If we are thinking, planning, or practicing known sin, it limits the effectiveness of our prayers (see Isa. 59:2; 1 Peter 3:7; James 5:16). We must remember, however, that we do not produce the righteousness required. We confess our sinfulness, ask for repentance, and surrender the will (not trying to do right by force of the will, but choosing to ask God to work in us). Then we must trust in His Word, not our feelings.

We are encouraged to pray for the lost (see 1 John 5:16), spiritual leaders (see 2 Thess. 3:1), and each other (see James 5:16). Job applied a blood sacrifice in behalf of his children (see Job 1:5). He prayed for his friends (42:8). In the case of his children, the head of the household bore the sins of the family and laid them on the innocent sacrifice. Satan held a legal claim against the wayward children due to their choices. These sins were borne by the father to Jesus through intercession. This intercessory work allows God to free the mind of children held captive by Satan when we pray.

> It were well for parents to learn from the man of Uz a lesson of steadfastness and devotion.... Amid the festivities of his sons and daughters, he trembled lest his children should displease God. As a faithful priest of the household, he offered sacrifices for them individually. He knew the offensive character of sin, and the thought that his children might forget the divine claims, led him to God as an intercessor in their behalf. (White, *Sons and Daughters of God*, p. 257)

> Children who have not experienced the cleansing power of Jesus are the lawful prey of the enemy, and the evil angels have easy access to them....By the faithful and untiring efforts of the parents, and the blessing and grace bestowed upon the children in response to the prayers of the parents, the power of the evil angels may be broken and a sanctifying influence shed upon the children. Thus the powers of darkness will be driven back. (White, *Counsels to Parents, Teachers, and Students*, p. 118)

> By sincere, earnest prayer parents should make a hedge about their children. They should pray with full faith that God will abide with them and that holy angels will guard them and their children from Satan's cruel power. (White, *Testimonies for the* Church, Vol. 7, pp. 42–3)

Abraham interceded for the inhabitants of Sodom and Gomorrah on the basis of expecting that not all were corrupt, countering Satan's claim that all those in Sodom had chosen him as their master. Moses asked that his own name be blotted out from the Book of Life if God could not save the Israelites who had fallen into blatant idolatry. This was a demonstration of unselfishness to the universe that refuted Satan's claims. It was a type of what Jesus went through on the cross.

Moses prayed for Miriam and Aaron. Daniel identified himself as a sinner when praying for his people. God looks for those who will intercede for sinners (see Isa. 62:6, 7; Jer. 5:1; Ezek. 22:30). We can refute the arguments of Satan by confessing that we are sinners by nature like those for whom we are praying, yet Christ's blood has been shed for us and the Holy Spirit has given us a heart sorrowful for sin. God has a right to do this for others as well. This is one way we feel repentance—by putting ourselves in their place. This may be part of the fervent, effectual prayer mentioned in James 5:16. This text in the Amplified Bible reads:

> Confess to one another therefore your faults (your slips, your false steps, your offenses, your sins) and pray [also] for one another, that you may be healed *and* restored [to a spiritual tone of mind and heart]. The earnest (heartfelt, continued) prayer of a righteous man makes tremendous power available [dynamic in its working].

The word translated "effectual" in the Greek means "having been energized." This makes one think of the fact that in the ancient sanctuary service, the sacrifices were ignited by divine fire. The devotion of effectual prayer comes from God. I believe that this devotion that comes from God in response to our request is an argument against the claims of Satan. The same word that is translated "effectual" in James 5:16 is the word translated "working" in the clause "faith working by love" (Gal. 5:6). The sense of the Greek here could be that faith has been supernaturally energized in or by love. It is when we dwell on the self-sacrificing love of God, as manifested on the cross, that our faith is energized. The Amplified Bible brings out some of this meaning: "For [if we are] in Christ Jesus, neither circumcision nor uncircumcision counts for anything, but only faith activated *and* energized *and* expressed *and* working through love."

When we focus on the cross of Christ, we receive this sacrificial love that increases our faith. As we eat the flesh and drink the blood of Christ, our faith is increased. Group prayer adds power to the argument against Satan. Matthew says, "Again I say to you that if two of you agree on earth concerning anything that they ask, it will be done for them by My Father in heaven" (18:19). Unity of spirit is a great catalyst for the operation of the Holy Spirit, for it demonstrates the power of salvation as nothing else. Jesus said, "By this all will know that you are My disciples, if you have love for one another" (John 13:35). In his last recorded prayer, He said, "And the glory which you gave me I have given them; that they may be one, even as we are one: I in them, and you in me, that they may be made perfect in one; and that the world may know that you have sent me, and have loved them, as you have loved me" (17:22, 23). The disciples were gathered in one accord when the Holy Spirit was poured out on the day of Pentecost (see Acts 2:1). This explains one reason why Satan tries so desperately to create division and discord.

Stories of Answered Intercessory Prayer

Mary met the pastor at the door after a series of evangelistic meetings. "I don't want anyone visiting in my home," she said. "I only attended these meetings because I am interested in a young man that was once an Adventist, but I have no intention of ever becoming one. I only wanted to know what kind of background he had when growing up."

The pastor honored her request, but put her name on his prayer list. The visitation team members prayed for her for a year. After one year, the pastor thought that she could not possibly object to a couple of the team members stopping by to invite her to meetings on prayer. Mary met them at the door saying, "I have to find out what I am supposed to do in order to join your church."

Mary said that she had a very vivid dream. In her dream, it was the darkest of nights. She heard a loud noise and the room began to shake. She dreamed that she got up out of bed and went to the window. There was a brilliant blazing light. She knew that Jesus was coming and she was not ready. She repeated, "I have got to know what to do in order to join your church."

Another pastor's talented son was rapidly gaining access to potential fame in the entertainment world. He was dipping into the lifestyle of the world. The pastor called church members forward to pray for their children week after week at church. The son is now a dedicated pastor, leading many to Christ.

Mike and Joan came into the prayer and counseling room at camp meeting. They were new Christians, fresh out of the world. They had been raised in Christian homes but were caught up with life in the fast lane. As they and their partying couples sought more and more excitement, they began experimenting with occult practices. It became a parlor game for the group to ask questions, and Joan's head would involuntarily nod yes or no. It was midnight and Joan was entertaining friends through fascinating communication with unseen guests when she and Mike looked at each other and said, "I don't think we should be doing this."

They were convicted that they should go home immediately. They picked up their Bibles and began to read. They were convicted that they should turn their lives over to Jesus. This camp meeting was the first step on their journey back to God from the occult. When Joan had called her mother to let her know what was happening, she discovered that at the very hour when she and Mike were struck with the conviction to stop, her mother had been on her knees pleading to God for her daughter and son-in-law.

Our prayers for the lost can be answered even

after we die. Trevor managed a service station. He was a man of the world. One night he lay on his bed drunk. He saw a being appear at the foot of his bed. The messenger told him he needed to stop drinking and start going to church or he would be forever lost. He was startled awake. Trevor stopped drinking and closed his service station on Sabbath. He attended church and asked to be baptized. He told the pastor that he was related to a well-known Seventh-day Adventist author. He knew that while a certain man and his wife were alive, they prayed earnestly for his soul.

As I write, I remember that I had a foot in the world with a heart set on football and worldly things. My dad ("Carl" in the opening chapter) took my name to the prayer meeting at church. Those prayers were answered. I found myself humming hymns, feeling a longing for a relationship with the Lord, and returning to God with my whole heart. I assured my dad that he had won at least his own son and others the Lord had drawn through his ministry.

Chapter 30
The Plague of Being Human

When Ted was attending the seminary, a masonry construction job became available for summer work. Faldo, Ted's boss, was concerned that the masons were standing around too long when they started a new job. They had to wait for the helpers to plug in electricity, hook up the hose, mix the mortar, and set up blocks. He thought that it would save money if they started the next job with mortar already mixed, so when they were leaving their morning job, he said, "Ted, mix a batch of mowta and put zher in zee veelbarrow so vee take to zee nex zyob." Realizing that it might harden on the way, he yelled, "And make it soupy. Make zher two."

Ted did as Faldo said. The wheelbarrow was filled to the brim with two batches of thin mortar. He wheeled it up a plank onto the high bed of the truck. When they arrived at the new jobsite, Faldo huffed and puffed around as was his custom, barking orders here and there. He was very stocky and moved quickly. "TED, GET ZHER DOWN ZAT VEELBARROW," he bellowed.

Ted saw that the truck bed was much higher than the ground on the new site and realized that the plank was too steep. "Faldo, that plank is awful steep and…"

"OH I GETZ IT MYSELF ZEN," Faldo yelled angrily. He scrambled up the plank and grabbed the handles with awesome force.

Ted stood with mouth hanging open as Faldo lurched backwards down the steep plank. He had no sooner started when the wheelbarrow developed a mind of its own. He had to run full speed backwards to keep out of its way. Faldo let out a great yell as he backpedaled furiously. He might have made it if there had been a clear path, but Drew, the head tender, had set a large tub in the yard. He used this to keep dry mortar ready to shovel into the mixer. Faldo fell smack down into the tub and the soupy mortar slopped over his belly as though he were taking a bath in it. Ted tried to pull him out, but in embarrassment Faldo moaned, "Jus leef me heah!" Fortunately, there was a corner of the house where Ted could go around to attend to some vital task, which, he shamefully admits, amounted to rolling on the ground with unsanctified laughter. When Ted went back, Faldo had cooled down enough to let him pull the wheelbarrow off and help him out. He was uncharacteristically quiet the rest of the day.

Faldo was a good man. He loved the Lord. He had amazing talents, but like the rest of us he was plagued with the fact that he was human. It could happen to any of us. We get in a hurry and our natural limitations place stumbling blocks in our way. To the unconverted, this human weakness is manifested in the indulgence of sinful desires and tendencies. I firmly believe that the thing that keeps millions from professing Jesus is that they somehow think they don't have what it takes to be a Christian. They need to realize that Jesus promises to change our natural human nature.

Ted's foreman, Klaus, had also come from the old country. He had been a professional boxer as a young man. He drank heavily on the weekends and came in Monday mornings looking for a fight with the world. His first words to Ted were, "I am going to give you a licking."

Ted made Klaus a matter of prayer and found ways to befriend him. He enjoyed his little folk songs and laughed with him when the foreman was in a good mood.

One day, Klaus and Ted were working alone on a chimney top. The house was close to Lake Michigan. Klaus shouted, "MUD!" This meant that he needed some mortar right away. Ted noticed a mournful foghorn sounding down near the lake, and as he walked over to get some mortar he said, "Must be pretty foggy down there on the water."

Klaus yelled, "That's not the only place it is foggy. I said MUD!" Ted laughed loudly and Klaus started to laugh at his own humor. It was an explosive, spontaneous laugh. When his mouth flew open, his pipe popped out and fell inside the chimney. His face dropped again and he angrily said, "Now you loose me my pipe down the shimly."

Still laughing, Ted replied, "Klaus, I told you I was going to get you to stop smoking." Klaus began to chuckle as well.

One day, it started to rain heavily and the men sat inside waiting for it to stop. Klaus and Drew began talking about how their kids were not going to bring women into the house when they became teens. They were not going to bring alcohol into the house either.

"I am puzzled about something," Ted remarked. "You men talk about doing those things yourselves, but don't want your kids to do them. Why is that?"

"Ven I vas young," Klaus answered, "All I knew vas falling bombs and var. I vont my kids to haf a better life."

"Have you ever thought that God feels the same way about you?"

Tears flowed freely down Klaus's cheeks as he said, "Ted, there is no hope for me." Klaus said that he could not help but lust after beautiful women, not to mention issues with the other commandments. What he was saying is that he did not find it within himself to be a Christian. Ted told Klaus that by nature he was just as mean and sinful as Klaus was. The difference was that he had a Savior. Klaus began taking Bible studies after that.

The point I am making is that Klaus had openly shared the concern of millions. For some the problem may be lusting after someone attractive. For others it could be love of money, pride, or worldliness. The bottom line is that to the unconverted, the words of the Calypso song are all so true: "If it is something you like, you can be certain that it's illegal, it's immoral, or it makes you fat." The devil plants the idea that Christians are those who by nature feel holy and trying to be a Christian would make one weak and take away their fun. The solution is for them to grasp the truth that Jesus died to save real sinners. Jesus will change human nature into the likeness of His divine nature if we ask. This is why soulwinning Bible studies begin with salvation as found in the gospel.

We were building a church in Russia near Magadan on the Siberian coast. We had received word that a group of Russian soldier guards in a prison wanted to hear us speak. We traveled by bus to a crude prison camp. It was difficult to breathe as hundreds of Russian military men crowded into a small, upstairs assembly room. Our conference president, Max Torkelsen, and I were chosen to speak. Max gave a good sermon on health. I tried to talk against the theory of evolution.

After we finished, the commander came up to us and through an interpreter said, "I thought you might be interested in what we would really like to know. Concerning health, why would any of us want to live longer? Life is miserable. Concerning origins, there are many theories. The latest one is that we spun off from some star. This is what we would really like to know. We understand that we have souls. The question is, what do we need to do to keep from burning in hell? And do we need to give up all our vices?"

Wow! If only we had known what the Holy Spirit had already accomplished in their lives. We left hundreds of Bibles, which were grabbed by hungry hearts and open hands. Conviction is the major thing that makes unbelievers uncomfortable. This is the area where the Holy Spirit brings about the greatest opportunities. It is the work of the Holy Spirit to convict of sin. It is equally the work of the Holy Spirit to bring comfort for sins forgiven.

The Holy Spirit will give insight concerning how to break through the layer of worldliness and indifference with which sinners hedge themselves in order to stifle conviction. Witnessing on the job involves understanding and a sense of timing that only the Holy Spirit can give. People of the world, in general, have respect for genuine Christians, but they judge us on the basis of what they expect us to be. Many unbelievers are ready to hold professed Christians to a very high standard. They are not impressed, however, with timid, passive, weak "holy Joes" who hold themselves aloof and censure others with self-righteous rebukes. It is their lack of comfort that leads them to taunt, tempt, and persecute Christians.

> **The Holy Spirit will give insight concerning how to break through the layer of worldliness and indifference with which sinners hedge themselves in order to stifle conviction.**

No matter what may be our work environment, there is often a mix of committed Christians and those who have either fallen away or never found the Lord. The principle of "A word in season to the one who is weary" applies here. The Holy Spirit will give an understanding and sensitivity as to how to approach the unbeliever in such a way that they do not feel defensive or condemned. Our personal testimony is the best way to do this. As someone has said, real witnessing is one beggar telling another beggar where to find food. We must first win their friendship and confidence that we are not out to relegate them to the lower regions or bring down fire upon their heads.

Men often enjoy good-natured banter. They probably know more than one would think about spiritual matters, though they may come across as crude and vulgar. One man expressed it well when he said, "I wouldn't mind going to church if people did not make me feel like a fool." It is that sense of self-condemnation that makes them uncomfortable around believers. Bible-thumping accusations drive them away or provoke them to retaliation. It is when they can identify with us and feel that we are genuinely interested in their wellbeing that men are most likely to respond to our testimony. When working with non-believing associates, determine what characteristics these people think makes a person a "good Joe." Try to manifest a few of those characteristics. Pray for the right time to share the story of your own need for forgiveness and cleansing.

On the job, it soon becomes apparent that some tasks are undesirable. Try to be willing to take more than your share of those jobs. On the construction site, there is often good-natured banter about whose turn it is to buy refreshments for the crew. Try to enter into the banter, but be willing to err on the benevolent side more than once.

Jerry worked a site with a carpenter construction crew. Their boss was a man by the name of Tozipilcco. The men told Tozipilcco that Jerry was a Seventh-day Adventist. The next day, as they were all sitting and eating lunch, Tozipilcco came bounding into the unfinished room. With great gusto he slid his lunch pail all away across the room and shouted, "Jerry, how come you Adventists won't carry guns and yet you take all the benefits that soldiers get for you by fighting?" It was unexpected and Jerry was put on the spot for sure. He tried to explain from Scripture that love is the most powerful force on earth and that the world's problems will never be solved by aggression and retaliation. To Jerry's surprise, Tozipilcco did not shout him down with ridicule or counter arguments. Jerry asked if that made sense. Tozipilcco listened and then quietly said, "Yes, but if I talked to some other Christian he would explain it another way."

The next day Jerry waited until all the men were seated, burst loudly into the room, slid his lunch pail across the room and shouted, "Tozipilcco, when are you going to go to church with me and find out what it is all about?"

Tozipilcco shot back, "Are you kidding. You are the only Adventist that I ever liked."

Tozipilcco was hungry for truth beneath his outward appearance of toughness. He felt more comfortable with banter than with silent condemnation. Some lunch hour jam sessions have been turned into Bible studies in much the same manner. An area manager in a large chain store studied with a number of co-workers who became baptized church members and then helped form the nucleus of a church plant.

Secular work environments are often filled with profanity and vulgar jokes. It is well to keep in mind the offender's need to feel important when responding to un-Christlike actions or talk. If possible, try to get the jump on them by telling really funny, clean jokes. When one of the construction workers started telling a joke that was obviously leading to profane thoughts, Ted put a hand on his shoulder and said, "Hey, I appreciate good humor. I am trying to be a Christian though, and have a hard time as it is. Please help me by telling clean jokes."

By appealing to his need rather than his righteousness, it was easier on other man's desire to feel important.

After mentioning this to the men on the job, the next day one of the men came running over to Ted, laughing, and said, "Here is one that Ted can hear." Ted later loaned that man *The Great Controversy* and they had good discussions about it.

It was easy to like Drew. He was raised in Oklahoma and had a country smile. He was good-natured and a hard worker. One day he and Ted sat eating lunch in Ted's car when Drew asked, "What do you think of them flyin' saucers?"

Ted reached for his Bible and turned to the book of Revelation where it talks about fire coming down from heaven and miracle-working powers that would deceive. The next day Drew wanted to eat together and talk more. Ted read Revelation 12 about the war in heaven and the fallen angels that appear as angels of light. Drew said, "I need to get my life straightened out." Ted told him that he thought he was already a Christian. He knew he attended church with his wife. Drew retorted, "Are you kiddin'? Do you think I would cuss like I do if I was a Christian?" He accepted Bible study material and gave his heart to the Lord.

Working men and women can be approached and won for the Lord if we allow the Holy Spirit to operate through us. The comfort of the Spirit gives strength and security so that the Christian is not intimidated by worldly mockery. It is the gospel that is the power of God unto salvation. Share your own need for forgiveness and cleansing. Tell others the way to find help. Explain how God was in Jesus receiving our hostility against Himself on the cross, and how He forgives and heals.

Chapter 31
More Powerful than Bullets

"My husband said he would shoot you if he ever saw you here, and that looks like his car coming up the drive." Sandra's words were shocking. The two female, volunteer Bible instructors and Pastor Fillmore looked out the window at the approaching vehicle. Sharon and Jane were part of the outreach team. They had been giving Bible studies to Sandra for several months. Sandra, her sister, and two older children studied faithfully. They responded positively to all the studies and marked their guides indicating a desire to be baptized and become members of the Seventh-day Adventist Church.

The time had come for the pastor to visit along with these two personal evangelists and prepare the Bible students for baptism. He had a sense that they were facing a struggle as they traveled down the road to Sandra's home. Sharon and Jane expressed some anxiety. The enemy does not give up easily and he always fights decisions. They spontaneously began singing, "Tis so sweet to trust in Jesus, Just to take Him at His word. Just in simple faith to trust Him, just to know, thus saith the Lord."

As they entered Sandra's home, they could feel that things were tense. She said that she decided not to be baptized now. When she told her husband, he erupted into a rage and told her he would divorce her if she joined the Seventh-day Adventist Church. He said that he did not want those women coming anymore, and if he ever saw the preacher there, he would shoot him on the spot.

You can always expect that the enemy will bring every form of opposition into play when it comes to soulwinning, especially at decision time. When people prepare to go witnessing, everything seems to be astir. Materials get mixed up. Maps get lost. Frustration often sets in. However, the enemy cannot prevent us from doing God's work. If we press on and do not let the distractions interfere, God and His angels will fight the battle for us. The witnessing group knew they were on God's errands and He would not allow the enemy to harm them unless, of course, it was time to lay down their lives in His service.

Pastor Fillmore was relieved, however, to see the automobile turn off the drive and onto the neighbor's lane rather than continue their way.

They quietly listened to Sandra's concerns and then said that they were not there to tell her what to do. All they could do was read the Bible with her. They read Matthew 10:32–39:

"Therefore whoever confesses Me before men, him I will also confess before My Father who is in heaven. But whoever denies Me before men, him I will also deny before My Father who is in heaven. Do not think that I came to bring peace on earth. I did not come to bring peace but a sword. For I have come to 'set a man against his father, a daughter against her mother, and a daughter-in-law against her mother-in-law'; and 'a man's enemies *will be* those of his *own* household.' He who loves father or mother more than Me is not worthy of Me. And he who loves son or daughter more than Me is not worthy of Me. And he who does not take his cross and follow after Me is not worthy of Me. He who finds his life will lose it, and he who loses his life for My sake will find it."

The gospel workers' hearts were heavy as they drove back to the church. Pastor Fillmore called the prayer chain and decided to fill the baptistery anyway in anticipation that the power of the Word would win out over the threat of the bullet.

When Sabbath morning arrived, all four family members were there ready for baptism. Sandra said, "My husband's bark is worse than his bite."

The baptism took place and the women continued to integrate the four new members into the church and disciple them in more outreach ministries.

This story underscores the fact that the power to convert is contained in the Scripture. It is not in our quantity of speaking or persuading. This is a secret that the beginner does not always grasp. As soul-winners, it is our part to be faithful and study with all who are receptive. We must make it our purpose, however, to let the Bible do the work. The same God who "spoke and it was done…commanded, and it stood fast" (Ps. 33:9) operates through His Word. "By the word of the Lord the heavens were made" (v. 6). Jesus cast out demons by the words of His mouth. He healed the lame, gave sight to the blind, and hearing to the deaf through His words. He raised the dead by the power of His word. He said, "The words that I speak to you are spirit, and *they* are life" (John 6:63). His word will not return to Him void.

For this reason, the gospel worker must guard against anything that might distract from planting the seed of the Word in the heart. Social conversations, great discussions, speculations, or even prayer must not take precedence over a study of the Word of God.

The Word of God is more powerful than bullets, even in areas of physical warfare.

Chapter 32

Fires of Pentecost on the Battlefront

Men with machine guns were lined up in front of a war-riddled, high-rise apartment building. They were prying open the barricaded doors on the bottom floor. Jon and I were on our way to witness door-to-door across the Green Line (no-man's land between fighting forces) in Beirut, Lebanon. Refugees were forcing their way into abandoned or semi-vacated apartment buildings facing the Green Line. This was three years after the beginning of the Lebanese civil war in which 120,000 people were killed.

Prior to our door-to-door visitation, we met for prayer early each morning for several weeks. We knew from past experience that God was not limited in what He could do to reach souls thirsting for the gospel.

Jon put together some guidelines on health issues related to the war situation. The paper read, "Do you find yourself feeling listless, having headaches, upset stomach or diarrhea? It is most likely the situation (war)." He then went on to explain that a diet rich in vitamin B would help, as well as how whole grains were a good source of vitamin B.

We inserted these inside *Signs of the Times* magazines and planned to distribute them door-to-door, beginning at apartments facing no-man's land. At that time, we did not know that we would be knocking on the doors of guerilla fighters and their families who had taken residence in the abandoned buildings.

As I climbed the dark stairway to the first door, I was met by the musty odor of wet, broken plaster and cement mingled with fragments of household contents strewn along the steps and hallways. Jon and I separated in order to cover more territory. I knew that I was not alone, however, for I claimed the promises spoken to Moses—"Now therefore, go, and I will be with your mouth and teach you what you shall say" (Exod. 4:12). Yet I felt apprehensive as I approached the first door.

We agreed to start at the top and work our way down the building. The closer I got to the top of the dark stairwell, the more I was convinced that no one could be living there. The stench of urine mingled with wet, broken mattresses and other charred debris. I had the urge to turn around and run down the stairs. I didn't know what to expect. I could not speak Arabic and not many spoke English. I hesitated as my eyes adjusted to the gloomy hallway. What would happen in this war-torn land? Fear lurked in every corner. I knocked. The sound echoed along the stark plaster walls of the dim corridor. Suddenly, there was a burst of light and a young man stood in the doorway. Adrenalin added a spring to my step. I popped forward and handed him the *Signs of the Times* with the insert on health. I said, "From America." He accepted the magazine and disappeared quickly behind the closing door.

When I knocked on the next door, an Arab woman answered. She was about thirty-five years old, short, plump, and pleasant looking. Her eyes brightened as she recognized the *Signs of the Times*. She was raised in a Seventh-day Adventist orphanage in Egypt and spoke English with an American accent. When I told her what I was doing, she replied, "I will go with you and translate for you." God paves the way in the most impossible situations. He miraculously helped solve the language barrier.

Now the four of us, my translator, and I, along with our two angels, went to the next apartment. The people invited us inside. It was a refugee family. A wife and daughter stayed in the background. Several sons gathered around the patriarch. Through the translator and broken English, he told me that they were displaced from their homeland by the expansion of "those people." He said there were many Christians in his home country. He sometimes went in to light fires for "those people" on their Sabbath. I was excited and foolishly tried speaking Hebrew with him.

Later my translator told me that a leader came by her home the week following my first contact. He said that the man (referring to me) who came in the building the previous week was a spy. He also said, "He even knew some of that language."

> **God paves the way in the most impossible situations. He miraculously helped solve the language barrier.**

She was able to tell him, "No! He is one like me" and explain the mission work of Seventh-day Adventists.

The refugee patriarch said that his family needed food. He was happy to receive the small assistance that I gave them from time to time. I had an Arabic Bible and could find the books, chapters and verses. I pointed to the texts and let them read. This accomplished two things: 1) It crossed the language barrier and 2) they read the Bible for themselves.

The following week, as I entered the hallway, Ahmed, the young commando whom I first encountered, was in the hallway. He yanked the *Signs* out of my hand and said loudly, "I want this!" He then followed me and joined the Bible study in the home of the refugee family. I believe he was a son-in-law.

Suddenly, during our study, Ahmed jumped to his feet, looked back and forth quickly, then said in English, "I want you to take me to America."

I sent up a quick prayer— "Lord how should I answer?"

"Ahmed, we have problems in America too. Just before we came here, thieves broke into my garage, took my chainsaw and other tools. There are many murders in the streets and robberies. Our only hope is for Jesus to come. What is it that you need?"

He replied, "I need a job." We knelt down and prayed that he could find a job.

The next week, Ahmed met me in the hallway. He was all smiles. Crossing his fingers and holding them high in the air, he beamed, "From diss day, me, Jesus like diss." When I asked what had happened, he replied, "I got a job."

He was repairing automobiles in the street. Right there on the edge of no-man's land, amidst the rubble, he found a man who had a repair business. Ahmed had a new confidence in the future.

He invited me to his apartment for an additional study. When I arrived, I found his small flat filled with young men. We followed the same method of study. We brought Arabic hymnals and sang the tunes while they read the words.

As I approached another apartment building, I was so startled as I, in the semi-darkness of the elevator hallway, looked into the face of a man so severely scarred from burns that I struggled to recognize him as a human being. His compassionate voice and helpful information told me he was one of God's own.

On the second floor of that building, a blonde, Caucasian woman invited us in for studies. She was from Germany, married to a local diamond dealer. Kristina told us how she looked out the window and saw a man pull a knife and kill another man over a dog. The dead man's body lay in the street for some time before anyone came and took it away. She added, "And the man that killed him lives right above us."

I asked, "Did the police come and arrest him?"

"No. They have machine guns and grenade launchers. The police can do nothing."

She was so upset by the war situation that she took her daughter to the beach to get away. Walking on the sand, she found a human arm that washed up on the beach.

Kristina was glad to study the Bible. She had questions from the "Unbelievers Bible" that was printed under atheistic jurisdiction. It took the Bible account and attacked, made fun of, or distorted it.

While these things were taking place, Jon was having his own adventure.

He first met Miriam. Distraught and perplexed by the war situation, she wanted to get away for prayers. As she was a member of the Druze religion, she went to the hills where there were religious shrines. She painfully and tearfully had made her way up the path, found a priest, and asked him to pray for her. He responded that he would not pray for her unless she gave him money. Since she did not have money to give, with hot tears flowing and a heart breaking with a longing for peace, she cried out to God and made her way back to the chaos of downtown Beirut. She was walking aimlessly down the street, trying to pray, when she looked up and saw my partner Jon. She later said that she perceived him as an angel. Upon approaching him and expressing her longing for prayer, Jon prayed for Miriam and started Bible studies with her.

Together, Jon and I ended up with five or six home groups with which to study. We felt that if we could bring together those who were studying, we would have enough to start a church. We were headed in that direction when the time came to leave Beirut. On my last few visits across the Green Line, a Lebanese pastor accompanied me to continue studying with the interested folks. Dwight Rose and his wife, Canadian missionary teachers at the church school, continued to study with Miriam. They started a home church in her house. She and members of her family were baptized.

We are now engaged in a spiritual battle of the highest magnitude. Physical conflict may break out around us at any moment. The Christian soldier is on the spiritual battlefront every day. Only the fires of Pentecost can meet the challenge of witnessing in the last days.

I share this story and those following, not because I think you should do as others have done, but to build confidence that God can work in any situation and His miracles are most often manifested amidst the most unlikely circumstances. You can experience soulwinning miracles in your own sphere of influence, even in secular-minded, gospel-hardened countries like the U.S.A.

Chapter 33
Getting Past the KGB

"Split the waters. Charge out into the rain!" The spine-tingling voice of Mike Fracker rang in my ear as his hulking frame brushed by and dashed out into the downpour. He had no umbrella or raincoat.

We were in Kiev, Ukraine. Rain was pelting down in huge globs and gushing off the sidewalk. Lightning flashed. A blast of thunder shook the building. I was dressed in a suit coat, as was Mike. I had no umbrella. The unprecedented task of mobilizing 500 Russians to go door-to-door in Kiev was so daunting that little details like weather escaped the mind until now. I looked at my partner, the Personal Ministries Director for the Russian Union Conference. He had no rain cover. I put my briefcase over my head and followed Mike into the cloudburst.

I will never forget what happened next. It was one of the most dramatic answers to prayer that I ever saw. We walked ten steps. The clouds split and rolled back like a scroll. The torrent stopped as if a mighty angel shut off a faucet. Sun brightened the walkway as golden fluid glistened on its way to the gutters.

Bright blue sky gleamed over the church as though suddenly covered by a great glass bubble. Black, ugly clouds churned from the ground to the top of a circle around the edges of the city. The clouds rolled like billows stayed by mighty hands. Walls of water from the Red Sea or River Jordan could not have been much more spectacular.

My Russian partner followed and we looked at each other in amazement. Water was still dripping off the sidewalk. We exclaimed loudly, almost in unison, "It's a miracle! It's a miracle!" However, that was only the beginning.

We were in the former Soviet Union in 1995 at the invitation of Russian church leaders. Fifty trainers from the U.S. were teamed together with Russian leaders to demonstrate how to start Bible studies door-to-door. The perfect storm was not the only barrier. Under Communism, one could suffer

> ***The clouds split and rolled back like a scroll. The torrent stopped as if a mighty angel shut off a faucet.***

exile or even death for openly sharing faith. Deeply ingrained in the Russian mindset was the thought that only trained theologians were equipped to give Bible studies. Russian pastors, let alone laypeople, had little if any training or experience in house-to-house evangelism. Language was a barrier.

We needed a woman on our team. We were to work together with a translator and a local person who would follow through with the Bible studies. This made a team of three to knock on doors. What Russian family would invite three strange men into their home? We made it clear to the 500 people who crowded into the Adventist Church that we should go out in groups of three that included both genders so that we would not frighten the people.

My Russian translator said that he had phoned one of his female relatives who lived in the area and that she would meet us at a certain place. She would follow through with the Bible studies. When we arrived at the designated street corner, however, we found that instead of a woman, our third member was a man. He was sent by his fearful wife. Now three big guys were left to go door-to-door. How could we ring doorbells without frightening the people? Time was running out and we would soon need to meet back at the church to lead out in the reporting. How would we find the targeted seven Bible studies?

Anxious to get back for reporting time, I pointed to an apartment house and said, "Let's go in there."

The men lowered their heads and whispered in Russian. Finally, my translator said, "This is the building of the KGB. Everyone who lives there is either a member of the KGB or a family member."

"Well, they need salvation also," I responded.

They talked together a few more minutes and then agreed. "We will go."

As an American, I had little realization of the risk they were taking. Russia could go back to an oppressive government at any time. They were putting their lives on the line, but they agreed to go.

"Americanski" was the only word I understood as we mingled with others who were entering inside the building. Attention was focused on the American in the group. We all crowded into an elevator that stopped on the first floor. We were laughing, talking, and trying to communicate. The people walked up to a door and rang the bell. The door opened and a woman welcomed them inside. She also motioned for us to enter. I thought this must be normal. When we got inside, everyone was seated and my translator introduced me and said that I had some questions. It was only then that they recognized that none of them knew us. It was a new thing for people to be able to give an opinion, so they were eager to share.

"Do you believe that there is a God?" I read from the sheet.

They looked at each other and talked a bit, then a spokesman said, "We don't know."

"Was Jesus just another man or was He God in flesh?"

Again, they talked and a spokesman said, "We know about Jesus but we do not know whether He was God or just another man." I then asked if they had read the Bible.

The spokesman said, "We have tried to read the Bible but we don't understand the words. We need someone to teach us."

I asked how many would like Bible studies. There were seven family groups and each one wanted to study the Bible. We handed out seven lessons and made arrangements to continue the studies.

When we got outside, my translator explained to me what happened. He said that it was a holiday and families came together to celebrate. The woman who invited us in thought we were with the family members who arrived at the same time. When this woman came to the realization of who we were, she recognized that a miracle took place. She then said to my translator, with a smile, "How did you get into my house? You are three men. You are dressed just like the mafia. I would never have let three men into my house." We went on our way rejoicing.

During two weekends that followed this training session, the fifty teams started more than 5,000 Bible studies all over the former Soviet Union. The goal was to form house churches. Some were in Muslim areas. We will not know the final results until eternity, though we understand that churches have been planted as a result, even among former Muslims.

Why do we not always see these kinds of miracles at home in the United States and other Western countries? I do not know, but I believe the same miracle-working God has promised to hear our prayers for those within our sphere of influence. I believe part of the answer may be that the Russians, as a nation, came to acknowledge their need. They realized that there was no future in humanism. It failed them in every way. How long will it be before the Western society comes to a similar conclusion?

Chapter 34
When the Rain Didn't Stop

Now what would we do? A foot of wet snow blanketed the ground and covered the sidewalks. Rain was falling. I had no boots or umbrella. We just finished a soulwinning rally in a rural church in Washington (state). I told them about our experience in Kiev where the Lord had stopped the rain. Now we looked out the window of our car and saw rain falling on the wet snow. We might be able to use umbrellas, but should I expect these dear folks to slog through wet snow without boots? I prayed and looked expectantly for the rain to stop, but it did not. The Lord has more than one way to answer prayer, however.

I continued to pray and drove to an apartment complex with covered walkways. The cover had kept the snow off the walks and now stopped the rain from falling on our heads. The people were receptive. One young woman came to the door and accepted the lessons. The church members faithfully visited during the following weeks with more Bible lessons. The woman invited a male friend to study with her. Together they completed the lessons and began attending church. The woman herself did not become a church member or continue the relationship with the young man. However, he continued to attend and was eventually baptized.

I never gave time to personal evangelism and not witness the Lord bless in spite of circumstances. When I served as pastor in a church in Oregon, we made a commitment to contact every home in the community and explain local community needs and the worldwide services of the Seventh-day Adventist Church. We had only a few blocks left to cover. Like in Kiev, a storm threatened. Wind blew the bills from my offering basket. I chased them down the street and asked the Lord to stop the rain. The sky opened up and the sun came out. On the very last street, our team met four people who accepted Bible studies and were later baptized.

On another occasion, my partner and I were following up media interest cards in Spokane. Contrary to what normally happens, there were no positive responses. People were not home, not interested, or simply wanted to talk or explain why they believed their way. I said to my partner, "I have never yet had a fruitless day of witnessing. This will be the first."

> **Whatever you do in the Lord's name, you can be sure that God will direct, protect, and provide positive outcomes.**

My partner said that there was one person who sent a card requesting Bible studies. He tried to reach the individual before, but could not get into the apartment. We drove to the apartment complex. A man stood at the door. He put a code into the lock and walked inside. We followed, not realizing what he did. We found the person for whom we were looking. She accepted Bible studies from my partner and his wife and was later baptized.

I am convinced the Lord will give results if one will set aside a two-hour block of time each week for focused, personal evangelism. Initially this time may be dedicated to prayer for the Holy Spirit and study. It may well expand to writing to, visiting, and associating with members of your *oikos*. You will eventually find Bible studies, books, or DVDs to loan. The Lord may lead you to accompany a church Bible worker, host a small group in your home, or be part of a church plant. Whatever you do in the Lord's name, you can be sure that God will direct, protect, and provide positive outcomes. The eternal rewards will be greater than we can ever imagine.

Chapter 35

Key Texts and Quotes:
The Baptism of the Holy Spirit and Witnessing (KJV)

Key Thought:

The baptism of the Holy Spirit brings assurance that we are sons and daughters of God. He gives a supernatural endowment that empowers our witness. A daily baptism gives us words to speak in season to the one who is weary (see Isa. 50:4). This involves placing the Word of God, through our testimony, in the heart of a receptive person at the right time. The Holy Spirit guides in this process.

What to Expect with the Baptism of the Holy Spirit

- Matt. 3:11—I indeed baptize you with water unto repentance: but he that cometh after me is mightier than I, whose shoes I am not worthy to bear: he shall baptize you with the Holy Ghost, and with fire:

- John 16:8–11—And when he is come, he will reprove the world of sin, and of righteousness, and of judgment: Of sin, because they believe not on me; Of righteousness, because I go to my Father, and ye see me no more; Of judgment, because the prince of this world is judged.

- John 16:6, 7—But because I have said these things unto you, sorrow hath filled your heart. Nevertheless I tell you the truth; It is expedient for you that I go away: for if I go not away, the Comforter will not come unto you; but if I depart, I will send him unto you.

- John 14:18—I will not leave you comfortless: I will come to you.

- John 14:26—But the Comforter, *which is* the Holy Ghost, whom the Father will send in my name, he shall teach you all things, and bring all things to your remembrance, whatsoever I have said unto you.

- John 15:26—But when the Comforter is come, whom I will send unto you from the Father, *even* the Spirit of truth, which proceedeth from the Father, he shall testify of me:

- Zech. 12:10—And I will pour upon the house of David, and upon the inhabitants of Jerusalem, the spirit of grace and of supplications:

and they shall look upon me whom they have pierced, and they shall mourn for him, as one mourneth for *his* only *son*, and shall be in bitterness for him, as one that is in bitterness for *his* firstborn.

- Rom. 8:16—The Spirit itself beareth witness with our spirit, that we are the children of God:

- Rom. 5:5—And hope maketh not ashamed; because the love of God is shed abroad in our hearts by the Holy Ghost which is given unto us.

What Is the Result of the Baptism of the Holy Spirit?

- Gal. 5:22, 23—But the fruit of the Spirit is love, joy, peace, longsuffering, gentleness, goodness, faith, Meekness, temperance: against such there is no law.

- Acts 1:8—But ye shall receive power, after that the Holy Ghost is come upon you: and ye shall be witnesses unto me both in Jerusalem, and in all Judaea, and in Samaria, and unto the uttermost part of the earth.

- Mark 13:11—But when they shall lead *you*, and deliver you up, take no thought beforehand what ye shall speak, neither do ye premeditate: but whatsoever shall be given you in that hour, that speak ye: for it is not ye that speak, but the Holy Ghost.

- Luke 4:18—The Spirit of the Lord *is* upon me, because he hath anointed me to preach the gospel to the poor; he hath sent me to heal the brokenhearted, to preach deliverance to the captives, and recovering of sight to the blind, to set at liberty them that are bruised,

- Acts 4:31—And when they had prayed, the place was shaken where they were assembled together; and they were all filled with the Holy Ghost, and they spake the word of God with boldness.

When you have received the baptism of the Holy Spirit, then you will understand more of the joys of salvation than you have known all your life hitherto. "Ye shall receive power, after that the Holy Ghost is come upon you; and ye shall be witnesses to Me…unto the uttermost parts of the earth." (White, *Manuscript Releases*, Vol. 5, p. 231)

How does this make a difference in your witnessing?

- Isa. 50:4—The Lord GOD hath given me the tongue of the learned, that I should know how to speak a word in season to *him that is* weary: he wakeneth morning by morning, he wakeneth mine ear to hear as the learned.

- John 15:26, 27—But when the Comforter is come, whom I will send unto you from the Father, *even* the Spirit of truth, which proceedeth from the Father, he shall testify of me: And ye also shall bear witness, because ye have been with me from the beginning.

- John 16:8—And when he is come, he will reprove the world of sin, and of righteousness, and of judgment:

- Acts 1:8—But ye shall receive power, after that the Holy Ghost is come upon you: and ye shall be witnesses unto me both in Jerusalem, and in all Judaea, and in Samaria, and unto the uttermost part of the earth.

- Jer. 1:9—Then the Lord put forth his hand, and touched my mouth. And the LORD said unto me, Behold, I have put my words in thy mouth.

- Rom. 14:17—For the kingdom of God is not meat and drink; but righteousness, and peace, and joy in the Holy Ghost.

- Rom. 15:13—Now the God of hope fill you with all joy and peace in believing, that ye may abound in hope, through the power of the Holy Ghost.

- 2 Cor. 1:12—For our rejoicing is this, the testimony of our conscience, that in simplicity and godly sincerity, not with fleshly wisdom, but by the grace of God, we have had our conversation in the world, and more abundantly to you-ward.

- 2 Cor. 6:10—As sorrowful, yet alway rejoicing; as poor, yet making many rich; as having nothing, and yet possessing all things.

Spiritual Gifts Qualified and Explained

- 1 Peter 4:11—If any man speak, *let him speak* as the oracles of God; if any man minister, *let him do it* as of the ability which God giveth: that God in all things may be glorified through Jesus Christ, to whom be praise and dominion for ever and ever. Amen.

- John 15:4—Abide in me, and I in you. As the branch cannot bear fruit of itself, except it abide in the vine; no more can ye, except ye abide in me.

- 1 Cor. 12:3–11—Wherefore I give you to understand, that no man speaking by the Spirit of God calleth Jesus accursed: and *that* no man can say that Jesus is the Lord, but by the Holy Ghost. Now there are diversities of gifts, but the same Spirit. And there are differences of administrations, but the same Lord. And there are diversities of operations, but it is the same God which worketh all in all. But the manifestation of the Spirit is given to every man to profit withal. For to one is given by the Spirit the word of wisdom; to another the word of knowledge by the same Spirit; To another faith by the same Spirit; to another the gifts of healing by the same Spirit; To another the working of miracles; to another prophecy; to another discerning of spirits; to another *divers* kinds of tongues; to another the interpretation of tongues: But all these worketh that one and the selfsame Spirit, dividing to every man severally as he will.

The promise of the Spirit is not appreciated as it should be. Its fulfillment is not realized as it might be. It is the absence of the Spirit that makes the gospel ministry so powerless. Learning, talents, eloquence, every natural or acquired endowment, may be possessed; but without the presence of the Spirit of God, no heart will be touched, no sinner be won to Christ. On the other hand, if they are connected with Christ, if the gifts of the Spirit are theirs, the poorest and most ignorant of His disciples will have a power that will tell upon hearts. God makes them the channel for the outworking of the highest influence in the universe. (White, *Christ's Object Lessons*, p. 328)

How does the Baptism of the Holy Spirit relate to the Latter Rain?

- Joel 2:28—And it shall come to pass afterward, *that* I will pour out my spirit upon all flesh; and your sons and your daughters shall prophesy, your old men shall dream dreams, your young men shall see visions:

- Acts 2:16, 17—But this is that which was spoken by the prophet Joel; And it shall come to pass in the last days, saith God, I will pour out of my Spirit upon all flesh: and your sons and your daughters shall prophesy, and your young men shall see visions, and your old men shall dream dreams:

[T]he latter rain will come, and the blessing of God will fill every soul that is purified from every defilement. It is our work today to yield our souls to Christ, that we may be fitted for the time of refreshing from the presence of the Lord--fitted for the baptism of the Holy Spirit. (White, *Selected Messages*, Book 1, p. 191)

What Part Does Surrender Play in the Baptism of the Holy Spirit?

- Acts 5:32—And we are his witnesses of these things; and *so is* also the Holy Ghost, whom

God hath given to them that obey him.

- Acts 2:1—And when the day of Pentecost was fully come, they were all with one accord in one place.

- James 5:16—Confess *your* faults one to another, and pray one for another, that ye may be healed. The effectual fervent prayer of a righteous man availeth much.

- Eph. 4:30—And grieve not the holy Spirit of God, whereby ye are sealed unto the day of redemption.

- Acts 7:51—Ye stiffnecked and uncircumcised in heart and ears, ye do always resist the Holy Ghost: as your fathers *did*, so *do* ye.

When the heart is emptied of self, it will be ready for the baptism of the Holy Spirit, and then you will be fitted to strengthen the sheep and lambs of the flock of Christ; for self will be hid with Christ in God. The Spirit of Christ will be manifested in your daily life. The apostle says, "Be ye holy in all manner of conversation." You are to be found without spot or wrinkle or any such thing. Your whole body, soul, and spirit are to be preserved blameless unto the coming of the Lord. What we need is the deep movings of the Spirit of God; for the standard of Christian life is expressed in these words: "Thou shalt love the Lord thy God with all thy heart, and with all thy soul, and with all thy mind, and with all thy strength....Thou shalt love thy neighbor as thyself." (White, *The Signs of the Times,* August 1, 1892, par. 5)

TEACH Services, Inc.
P U B L I S H I N G

We invite you to view the complete
selection of titles we publish at:
www.TEACHServices.com

We encourage you to write us
with your thoughts about this,
or any other book we publish at:
info@TEACHServices.com

TEACH Services' titles may be purchased in
bulk quantities for educational, fund-raising,
business, or promotional use.
bulksales@TEACHServices.com

Finally, if you are interested in seeing
your own book in print, please contact us at:
publishing@TEACHServices.com

We are happy to review your manuscript at no charge.

www.ingramcontent.com/pod-product-compliance
Lightning Source LLC
Chambersburg PA
CBHW080251170426
43192CB00014BA/2637